WAR HEROES OF FERNDOWN IN TWO WORLD WARS

BEYOND BRAVERY

IAN R DALE

© Ian R Dale, 2016

Edited by: Carol Waterkeyn

Published by The Royal British Legion – Ferndown Branch

Any views or opinions expressed in this publication are solely those of the author and may not represent those of the Royal British Legion.

Every attempt has been made by the author to secure the appropriate permissions for material reproduced in this book. If there has been any oversight, please contact the author in the first instance.

A CIP catalogue record for this book is available from the British Library.

ISBN 978-0-9955651-0-4

Book layout and cover design by Clare Brayshaw

Prepared and printed by:

York Publishing Services Ltd
64 Hallfield Road
Layerthorpe
York YO31 7ZQ

Tel: 01904 431213

Website: www.yps-publishing.co.uk

WAR HEROES OF FERNDOWN
IN TWO WORLD WARS

BEYOND BRAVERY

'To the memory of the fallen and the future of the living'

PROCEEDS FROM THIS BOOK WILL GO TO THE
ROYAL BRITISH LEGION WELFARE FUND

CONTENTS

Introduction	vi
Acknowledgements	viii
The Exhortation	xi
Part One: 1914–18 'The Great War'	1
Part Two: 1939–45 The Second World War	29
Appendix 1: Regiments from the War Memorial	49
World War I	50
World War II	70
Appendix 2: War memorials and cemeteries	79
World War I	80
World War I and II	120
World War II	124
Statistical information	143
Index of names	145
About the author	148

INTRODUCTION

During the monthly committee meeting of The Royal British Legion, Ferndown Branch in January 2014, discussions turned to the commemoration of the 100th anniversary of the start of the Great War on 4th August, and the 70th anniversary of D-Day on 6th June.

I have a great interest in family history, having researched my own family over the last 10 years or so. On looking at the War Memorial in the Remembrance Garden outside the Ferndown Branch in Church Road, it struck me that there was no information on those whose names appear, which makes them rather impersonal, instead of revealing the real people who gave their lives for their Country.

I then suggested to the committee that I research these names and provide a document to be used during the remembrance commemorations. This I did over the next few months and the documents have now been produced.

At the National Conference of the Legion in Torquay in May 2014, we met a group from Devon who have produced a book relating to all who served in the Great War from their area. This had cost some £16,000 to produce; an amount that could not be raised in our area.

Consequently, the idea of a short essay giving more detail on the names on the Memorial was conceived, and here it is.

It has been a labour of love for me and a very emotional one as well. I feel sure, as you read it, you will share my feelings for those brave souls, some so young, who died so that we may be free.

There are many books and poems written about the two wars and I have included just three which seem relevant to this essay. *The Exhortation* is said at every gathering of The Royal British Legion, the *Kohima prayer* is said at all remembrance gatherings, and the poem, *In Flanders Fields* is a particular favourite of mine and I make no apology for including it here.

ACKNOWLEDGEMENTS

In doing my research I have called upon the resources of Ancestry.co.uk, to which I have been a subscriber for many years. Forces War Records is another website that I have subscribed to in order to obtain a great deal of data. The Commonwealth War Graves Commission website has provided much information on the burial places and memorials to the fallen. I would like to thank them for their permission to reproduce this material.

Other websites have also provided data where the main ones were lacking in detail.

I must say a special thank you to the members of the Branch Committee, particularly Grant Parrott, for their help, criticism and guidance in the preparation of all the information in the memorial documents. Thanks also to Gwendolin Wells, niece of Percy Dacombe and Edward Hiscock, for the additional information and to Tony Amos for additional photographs. Thanks must also go to Margaret Parrott, Pat and Johnny Sturman, and Debbie Holden for proofreading and comments. A special thank you must go to my lovely wife, Irene, whose patience, constructive criticism and encouragement helped me through the more difficult moments in this work. Finally, I would wholeheartedly like to thank Ferndown Town Council, East Dorset District Council, and Sainsbury's for their kind donations, which enabled this book to be published.

Rather than present a clinical list of those who died as they appear on the memorial, I have presented the names in the order in which they died.

I have added, as appendices, the information on the regiments in which our heroes served, and the burial sites, war cemeteries and memorials are also listed.

NOTE

As with any published document, the War Memorial is subject to error; from typography to spelling, to possible mistaken identity. I have tried to correct the errors that I have found but, some leave me totally perplexed – RC March in the Second World War is a good example. My only source of information on these brave soldiers, sailors and airmen is from official records and consequently there may be a small amount of conjecture in the results.

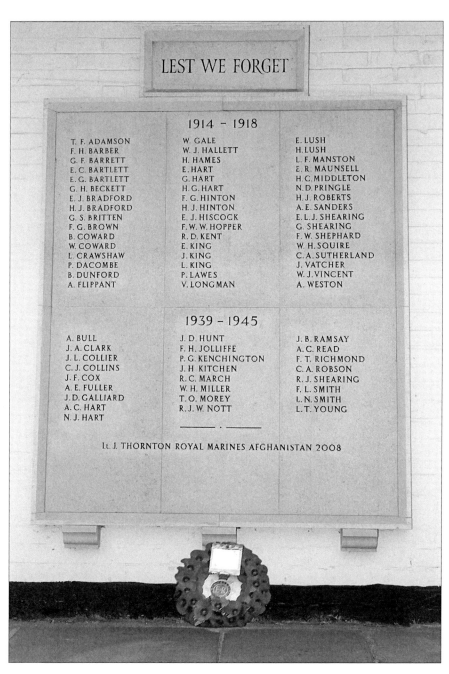

LEST WE FORGET

1914 – 1918

T. F. ADAMSON	W. GALE	E. LUSH
F. H. BARBER	W. J. HALLETT	H. LUSH
G. F. BARRETT	H. HAMES	L. F. MANSTON
E. C. BARTLETT	E. HART	E. R. MAUNSELL
E. G. BARTLETT	G. HART	H. C. MIDDLETON
G. H. BECKETT	H. G. HART	N. D. PRINGLE
E. J. BRADFORD	F. G. HINTON	H. J. ROBERTS
H. J. BRADFORD	H. J. HINTON	A. E. SANDERS
G. S. BRITTEN	E. J. HISCOCK	E. L. J. SHEARING
F. G. BROWN	F. W. W. HOPPER	G. SHEARING
B. COWARD	R. D. KENT	F. W. SHEPHARD
W. COWARD	E. KING	W. H. SQUIRE
L. CRAWSHAW	J. KING	C. A. SUTHERLAND
P. DACOMBE	L. KING	J. VATCHER
B. DUNFORD	P. LAWES	W. J. VINCENT
A. FLIPPANT	V. LONGMAN	A. WESTON

1939 – 1945

A. BULL	J. D. HUNT	J. B. RAMSAY
J. A. CLARK	F. H. JOLLIFFE	A. C. READ
J. L. COLLIER	P. G. KENCHINGTON	F. T. RICHMOND
C. J. COLLINS	J. H KITCHEN	C. A. ROBSON
J. F. COX	R. C. MARCH	R. J. SHEARING
A. E. FULLER	W. H. MILLER	F. L. SMITH
J. D. GALLIARD	T. O. MOREY	L. N. SMITH
A. C. HART	R. J. W. NOTT	L. T. YOUNG
N. J. HART		

Lt. J. THORNTON ROYAL MARINES AFGHANISTAN 2008

The Royal British Legion Memorial, Ferndown

THE EXHORTATION

THEY SHALL GROW NOT OLD

AS WE THAT ARE LEFT GROW OLD;

AGE SHALL NOT WEARY THEM,

NOR THE YEARS CONDEMN.

AT THE GOING DOWN OF THE SUN

AND IN THE MORNING

WE WILL REMEMBER THEM.

The Exhortation is an extract from a poem written by Robert Laurence Binyon called *For the Fallen*.

PART ONE:

1914–1918 WAR 'THE GREAT WAR'

IN AFFECTIONATE AND GRATEFUL MEMORY
OF PARISHIONERS—NAVAL AND MILITARY—WHO FELL
IN THE GREAT STRUGGLE OF THE NATIONS
IN THE CAUSE OF RIGHT AGAINST MIGHT.

1914 — 1918

LT COLONEL R . DAWSON KENT.D.S.O. 4.YORKS.
CAPTAIN E.RICHARD MAUNSELL. R.DUBLIN FUSILIERS.
CAPTAIN NORMAN D.PRINGLE. 6.EAST YORKS.
CAPTAIN ARTHUR E.SANDERS. YORK AND LANCS.
LIEUT.TRAVERS F.ADAMSON. DEVON.
LIEUT.HENRY J.ROBERTS. 6.DORSET.
2.LIEUT.WILLIAM J.VINCENT. ⅕.DORSET.

DUNFORD B	CORPORAL	K.R.R.C.	COWARD W	PRIVATE	2.DORSET
SUTHERLAND CA	CORPORAL	A AND S.H	DACOMBE P	"	R.A.S.C.
HISCOCK E.J	L.CORPORAL	9.DEVON	HAMES H	"	6.DORSET
SHEARING E.L.J	L.CORPORAL	7.HANTS	HART G	"	14.WORCESTER
WESTON A	PETTY OFFR	H.M.S GENESTA	HART H.G	"	5.WILTS
HART E	STOKER 1ST CL	H.M.S FIREDRAKE	HINTON H.J	"	2.DORSET
BRADFORD H.J	GUNNER	R.G.A	HOPPER F.W.W	"	OXF AND BUCKS
CRAWSHAW L	GUNNER	R.F.A	KING E	"	5.DORSET
HALLETT W.J	GUNNER	R.G.A	KING J	"	2.HANTS
MIDDLETON H.C	GUNNER	R.F.A	KING L	"	6.DORSET
HINTON F.G	M.GUNNER	6.DORSET	LAWES P	"	2.DORSET
FLIPPANT A	SAPPER	R.E	LONGMAN V	"	OXF AND BUCKS
SQUIRE W.H.N	PIONEER	R.E	LUSH E	"	2.HANTS
BARBER F.H	PRIVATE	6.DORSET	LUSH H	"	1.DORSET
BARTLETT B.E.G	"	1.DORSET	MANSTON L.F	"	8.CANADIAN
BARTLETT E.C	" SGE	1.DORSET	GALE W	"	C.G
BECKETT C.H	"	4.HANTS	SHEARING G	"	3.WILTS
BRADFORD E.J	"	5.DORSET	SHEPHARD F.W	"	3.DORSET
BRITTEN G.S	"	15.CHESHIRE	VATCHER J	"	K.R.R.C
BROWN F.G	"	7.DORSET	WOOLRIDGE J	"	K.O.YORKS L.I.
COWARD B	"	3.DORSET			

"WAXED VALIANT IN FIGHT." HEBREWS XI.34.

The Memorial inside Hampreston (All Saints) Church

LUSH, HERBERT 1884–1914

Our first casualty was Private Herbert Lush of the 1st Battalion Dorsetshire Regiment, the local regiment to which many of our names were attached (see appendix 1). Herbert was born in Wareham, Dorset in April 1884 to Silas and Augusta Lush, who moved to Ferndown soon afterwards. They are listed in this area in 1901. Herbert had four siblings; Cyril, born 1880, Harold, born 1882, Mabel, born 1886 and Olive, born in 1901. Herbert married Annie Elizabeth Froud (born July 1886) in February 1909 in Wimborne. He was working as an assistant to a baker and grocer in the 1911 census and the couple lived in Albert Road, Ferndown. In the listings of Herbert's service, Annie is recorded as living at 8, Elmes Road, Moordown, after his death.

The First Battalion was involved as part of the British Expeditionary Force from the very start of the war. They were at the Battle of Mons and subsequent retreat, the Battle of Le Cateau and the Affair of Crepy-en-Valois, the Battle of the Marne, the Battle of the Aisne, where Herbert died, the battles of La Bassée and Messines 1914, and the First Battle of Ypres. He was in the Departement de L'Aisne in Picardie, northern France when, on 9th September 1914 at the age of 30, he was killed in action – the common term for dying on the battlefield.

Herbert is buried at Montreuil-Aux-Lions British Cemetery (see appendix 2).

BARTLETT, BERTIE 1896–1914

Private Bertie Ernest George Bartlett, also of the 1st Dorsetshire Regiment (see appendix 1), was born in November 1896 in Kinson, Bournemouth, the son of Jesse and stepson of Lily Ellen King. According to records, they resided in 1914, at Black Cottage, Stapehill, Wimborne.

Bertie died with the British Expeditionary Force in 'France & Flanders' on 22nd October 1914 aged only 18, and is listed as killed in action.

Sadly, Bertie's body was probably never identified and he is listed on the Le Touret Memorial in Pas-de-Calais in France (see appendix 2).

DUNFORD, BERT 1889–1914

Rifleman Corporal Bert, or Bertie Dunford served with 3rd Battalion The Rifle Brigade (see appendix 1) and was born in Wimborne in 1889, the son of John Dunford. I could not find details of his mother. They do not appear in the 1911 census in Wimborne, but there is an entry in Ferndown (District 3) for this name.

The Rifles took part in the Attack on Ploegsteert Wood, which is where Bert was killed on 23rd October 1914 at the age of 25. His name appears on the Ploegsteert Memorial, which is approximately 7 miles south of Ieper (Ypres) in Belgium (see appendix 2).

ROBERTS, JOHN HENRY CHARLES (?)–1915

The memorial lists Lieutenant Henry J Roberts of the 6th Dorsetshires, (see appendix 1), sadly of whom I can find no record. However, I have found a Second Lieutenant of the 1st Dorsetshire regiment, who is the only one listed. Roberts is a fairly common name, so to find a close match, if not exact, is perhaps acceptable.

SUTHERLAND, COLIN ALLISTER 1897–1915

Private Colin Allister Sutherland of the 1st Battalion Argyll & Sutherland Highlanders (see appendix 1) was born in Wimbledon, Surrey on 31st July 1897. He was the son of William Colin Sutherland MA and Daisy Gwendolin Bloomfield Sutherland. They had moved to 'Stour Bank' Little Canford, Wimborne by 1911, and 'Green Brae', Colehill, Wimborne by the time Colin died.

Colin enlisted on 7th September 1914, lying about his age, as many did. His enlistment document is published online and clearly shows that he entered July 1895 as his date of birth, claiming to be two years older than he actually was, as shown in the birth records available now. His regiment was fighting in the Battle of Ypres when he was killed in action on 9th May 1915, at the age of 18. Colin's name appears on the Ypres (Menin Gate) Memorial in West Vlaanderen, Belgium (see appendix 2).

KING, JOHN ALBERT 1889–1915

Private John Albert King of 2nd Battalion Royal Hampshire Regiment (see appendix 1) was born in Weymouth, Dorset in May 1889 to Samuel and Charlotte King. John married Lily Passmore in May 1910 and they lived at 2, New Borough in Wimborne. He was a Postman.

The Hampshires mobilised for war and embarked from Avonmouth, Bristol to go to Alexandria, Egypt then on to Gallipoli, Turkey. The regiment was involved in the battles for Krithia and the Achi Baba Heights, during which John was killed on 28th April 1915, aged 25. John's name appears on the Helles Memorial (see appendix 2), on the tip of the Gallipoli peninsula.

PRINGLE, NORMAN DOUGLAS 1884–1915

Captain Norman Douglas Pringle of 6th Battalion East Yorkshire Regiment (see appendix 1) was born in Pencoed, Bridgend, Glamorganshire in May 1884 to Henry Tumbrill and Janie Isabella Pringle. Norman was the fourth of five children; Arthur, Gladys, Kenneth, Norman and Mara. In 1901 he was a student boarder at St George's, Campden Hill, Kensington, London. By 1911, Norman was living with his father and stepmother, Naomi, in 'Hawtree', Ferndown, Dorset. He was, by then a Divinity Student.

Norman joined the East Yorkshire Regiment. The 6th battalion mobilised and left from Avonmouth via Mudros for Gallipoli. They landed at Suvla Bay on 1st July 1915 and were involved in several actions against the Ottoman Empire, during which, on 7th August 1915 at Suvla Bay he was killed in action at the age of 31. Like John King, his name appears on the Helles Memorial in Gallipoli (see appendix 2).

BRADFORD, EDWARD 1895–1915

Private Edward George Bradford of the 5th Battalion Dorsetshire Regiment (see appendix 1), was a local boy, born in Canford, Dorset in January 1895 to William and Lily Louisa Bradford. From 1901 to 1911 the family lived at the Fox & Hounds Public House in Little Canford (just off the Canford Bottom Roundabout). By 1914 they were at Stapehill Farm, Wimborne. Edward was employed locally as a gardener.

The 5th Battalion, like the 6th, went to Gallipoli but left from Liverpool travelling via Mudros and Imbros. They landed at Suvla Bay and the following day, Edward died in action on 8th August 1915 aged just 20. His name also appears on the Helles Memorial in Gallipoli (see appendix 2).

KING, ERNEST 1895–1915

Private Ernest King of the 5th Battalion Dorsetshire Regiment (see appendix 1) was born in Colehill in October 1895, the middle one of the three sons born to Samuel and Charlotte King. The family lived at 'Baker Cottage' Canford Bottom.

In August 1915, the 5th Battalion landed in Suvla Bay in Gallipoli with the aim of breaking the deadlock in Gallipoli at that time. This landing was intended to give support to the breakout of the Anzac sector. However, it made little difference and after a week of indecision and inactivity, on 15th August 1915 the Commander in Chief, Lieutenant General Sir Frederick Stopford was dismissed. He is blamed for the failure of this campaign. Just four days later on 19th August, Ernest was killed in action at the age of 19. His name appears on the Helles Memorial on the Gallipoli peninsula as well (see appendix 2).

LAWES (OR LAWS), JOHN PHILLIP 1893–1915

Private John Phillip Lawes of the 2nd Battalion Dorsetshire Regiment (see appendix 1) was born in St Pancras, London in November 1893 to John and Harriet Lawes, the third of six children. By 1911, Phillip (as he now called himself) was a boarder in Church Road, Ferndown and worked as a labourer.

The Second Battalion was deployed to the Persian Gulf in November 1914 as part of the 16th Brigade under Brigadier General Delamain. After landing at Fao beach, they were immediately fighting the Ottomans to gain control of the fortress. This they achieved after four days of hard, hand-to-hand battle. It was during the push towards Baghdad that Phillip was killed in action on 12th September 1915 at the age of 21. His name appears on the Basra Memorial (see appendix 2).

CRAWSHAW, LESLIE 1897–1915

Gunner Walter Leslie Crawshaw of the Royal Field Artillery, 'C' Battery, 87th Brigade (see appendix 1), was born in February 1897 in Sedgehill, Wiltshire, to James and Rosa Crawshaw.

By 1911 Walter was living at East Martin Farm in Martin, near Salisbury, where he also attended school. At the time of his death his parents were living at 5, Victoria Road, Ferndown. The Royal Field Artillery were fighting on the Western Front all through the war and Leslie was fatally wounded. He died on 23rd September 1915 and was buried in the Merville Communal Cemetery in northern France (see appendix 2).

BROWN, FREDERICK GEORGE 1898–1916

Private Frederick George Brown of the 7th Battalion of the Dorsetshire Regiment (see appendix 1) was born in April 1898 in Hampreston to John and Emily Brown, and was the eldest of three children. John was a farmer and the family lived in 'Sunnyside' in Ferndown.

Although Frederick would have worn the badge of the Dorsetshire Regiment, he was a conscripted soldier and was sent to the 35th Training Reserve Battalion, which was how recruits were trained in the later stages of the war. I cannot find out what caused his death, but he died at home in Ferndown on 26th February 1916 at the age of just 18. He is buried in Weymouth Cemetery in Dorset (see appendix 2).

SANDERS, ARTHUR EDWARD 1887–1916

Captain Arthur Edward Sanders of the 2nd Battalion Yorkshire & Lancaster Regiment (see appendix 1) was born in London's Hanover

Square in July 1887 to William and Louise Elizabeth Sanders. They remained in London until at least 1911 where the census shows them residing at 3, Upcerne Road, Chelsea. Arthur was a Timber Merchant's clerk.

At the time of Arthur's death, his parents were living in 'Hillcrest', Ferndown, Dorset. The Yorkshire and Lancashire Regiment Second Battalion was involved in the Battles of Flers-Courcelette, Morval and Le Transloy, during one of which, on 19th May 1916, Captain Sanders was killed in action at the age of 18. He is buried in the Poperinghe Military Cemetery in West Vlaanderen (see appendix 2), Belgium. This cemetery is in three parts, as it overflowed with all the casualties from Ypres (now called Iepers) and Captain Sanders is in the 'new' cemetery, opened in 1915.

MAUNSELL, EDWIN RICHARD LLOYD 1892–1916

Captain Edwin Richard Lloyd Maunsell of the 1st Battalion Royal Dublin Fusiliers (see appendix 1), was born in Bothwell, Lanarkshire, Scotland in January 1892. His parents were Major John Drought Maunsell (born in Ireland and retired from the Army Pay Corps) and Euphemia Sullivan Maunsell. They lived in Taunton, Somerset. By 1911, they had moved and were living at 'Ballywilliam', Dudsbury Avenue, Longham, Wimborne.

Edwin was by this time in the Royal Dublin Fusiliers, holding the rank of Second Lieutenant. During 1916 he was evacuated from Gallipoli due to the high casualty numbers and disease and was sent to Egypt. After a couple of months, they were moved again, this time to the Somme, where they were involved in the battles of Albert and Transloy Ridges. In one of these, Captain Maunsell was killed in action on 1st July 1916 at the age of 24 and was later buried in the Auchonvillers Military Cemetery (see appendix 2), in France.

ADAMSON, TRAVERS FARRANT 1895–1916

Second Lieutenant Travers Farrant Adamson of the 9th Battalion Devonshire Regiment (see appendix 1) was born in Forest Hill, south east

London on 2nd July 1895 to Travers Patrick Muirhead Adamson and Ethel Adamson; Travers was one of four children. His father was an accomplished Australian artist who died at the age of 41 in 1901. Travers's mother Ethel (née Farrant) was the daughter of a surgeon in Exeter. Travers was christened on 15th August 1895 in Christ Church, Forest Hill. The family moved to Cornwall before 1901 and are listed there in that year's census as living at 1, Penare, Penzance. By 1911 the widowed Ethel was living at Albany Terrace, St. Ives, Cornwall and the young Travers was at boarding school in St John's College in Hurstpierpoint, Sussex.

Travers Adamson's battalion was fighting in France and was involved in the battles of Albert, Bazentin, High Wood, Delville Wood and Guillemot. It was during one of these that Travers was killed in action on his 21st birthday. At the time of his death, his family were living at 'Corleone', Longham, Wimborne. Travers is buried in the Devonshire Cemetery in Mametz in the Somme in France (see appendix 2). One other document came to light, which showed that he had left an estate of £681, which was to be shared between two of his younger siblings.

HART, EDWARD CLIFFORD FRANK 1890–1916

Private Edward Clifford Frank Hart, of the 1st/4th Battalion Hampshire Regiment (see appendix 1) was born in September 1890 to Richard and Ellen Hart in Canford Magna, Dorset, Edward being the youngest of seven children. By 1901, Ellen was widowed, now with another child and the two eldest no longer living at home. By 1911, Edward was a teacher, boarding in Lyme Regis at 10, Church Street.

In 1915 the Hampshires were in Basra, Iraq and were fighting alongside a number of Indian Divisions when Edward was killed doing his duty on

11th July 1916 aged 26. He is buried in the Amara War Cemetery (see appendix 2) on the left bank of the Tigris in Iraq.

LUSH, THOMAS EUGENE 1892–1916

Private Thomas Eugene (known by his second Christian name) Lush of the 2nd Battalion Hampshire Regiment (see appendix 1) was born in Wareham, Dorset in August 1892 to Silas and Augusta Lush. He was the youngest of their four children. By 1901, Silas and family were living in Longham, Dorset, where Silas was a shoemaker and Eugene was a scholar.

By 1911 Eugene was living in Piddletrenthide, Dorset where he was a baker. The Second Battalion was in France and Flanders in 1916 and during his service they were involved in the Battles of Albert and Transloy Ridge. Eugene was fatally wounded and died on 10th August 1916 at the age of 24. He is buried in the Lijssenthoek Military Cemetery (see appendix 2) in Belgium.

COWARD, WILLIAM 1891–1916

Private William Coward of the 2nd Battalion Dorsetshire Regiment (see appendix 1) was born in Wimborne in August 1891. His parents were Albert John and Fanny Coward. William was their third of six children. Albert was a brickmaker and the family lived on Ringwood Road, Longham. I could not find William on the 1911 census, which suggests that he had already joined up.

With the 2nd Battalion, William was sent first to India and then to the Middle East. By September 1916, the battalion was deployed as part of the defence force on the Tigris River. It was on 2nd September that William was killed in action at the age of 25. At the time of writing I could not find his burial location, but others of this regiment are named on the Basra Memorial (see appendix 2).

HALLETT, WALTER JAMES 1894–1916

Gunner Walter James Hallett of the 25th Heavy Battery, Royal Garrison Artillery (RGA) (see appendix 1) was born in Corfe Mullen in Dorset in November 1894 to James and Sarah Ann Hallett. Walter was the eldest of four children. In 1901 they were all living in Pamphill, James being a farm carter. By 1911 they had moved to Wareham, where James and Walter were both farm carters. By the time of Walter's death, the Halletts were living at 335, Little Canford, Wimborne.

The Royal Garrison Artillery that Walter had joined was a branch of the Royal Artillery and provided the heavy firepower behind the lines. When you hear of the heavy guns and howitzers 'pounding' the enemy from behind the lines, this would be the RGA. Walter was killed while performing his duty on 11 September 1916 in the Somme aged just 21. He is buried in the Englebelmer Communal Cemetery (see appendix 2) in France.

WESTON, ARTHUR 1885–1916

Petty officer Arthur Weston of the Royal Navy was born in Chiseldon, Wiltshire in 1885. Arthur married Rose Ellen Dominey in July 1913. The couple lived on Wimborne Road, Ferndown.

Arabis class Sloop HMS Genista

Arthur served aboard HMS *Genista*, an Arabis class minesweeping sloop which had been launched on 26th February 1916. She was one of the 36 'Flower class' ships that were built with urgency under the Emergency War Programme. *Genista* was on minesweeping patrol in the north Atlantic, off Ireland, when she was torpedoed by German Submarine U-57 on 23rd October 1916 and sunk with the loss of 61 of the 73 men onboard. Arthur was 31 years old. The submarine had previously launched on 29th April 1916, was responsible for sinking over 100,000 tons of shipping, and finally surrendered on 24th November 1918.

SHEARING, GEORGE 1898–1917

Private George Shearing of 98th Company Machine Gun Corps (see appendix 1) and not the Wiltshire Regiment as listed on the Memorial, was born in Ringwood, Hampshire in April 1898. His father and mother were Samuel and Sarah Shearing. George was their fourth child of five. In 1901 they were living in Ferndown and by 1911 resided at Victoria Road, Ferndown. This may not have been a move, merely the 1911 Census being more detailed.

Members of the Machine Gun Corps saw a great deal of action in the war and the soldiers were in every theatre. George's 98th Company was at the Somme in 1917 when he was killed in action on 16th February 1917, aged only 19. He was laid to rest in the Bray Military Cemetery (see appendix 2) just outside Bray-sur-Somme in France.

Note: The Wiltshire Regiment had no soldier serving throughout the Great War with the name 'Shearing'. This man lived in Ferndown thus qualifying him to be on the memorial, so I present him here.

HINTON, FRANK GEORGE 1895–1917

Private Frank George Hinton of the 6th Battalion Dorsetshire Regiment (see appendix 1) was born in Wimborne in February 1895, the eldest of four children, to George Charles Hinton and Emily Ursula Hinton. They lived at 160, Stapehill, Ferndown. George was a labourer in a nursery on the 1901 census and by 1911, Frank had joined him. I cannot find any nurseries listed in the 1911 census, so I am unsure where it was.

During his service, Frank was a Machine Gunner and the battalion was fighting various battles; the first and second of Scarpe, in the capture of Rouex, and the first and second of Passchendaele. Frank was killed in action on 18th February 1917, aged 22. He is listed on the Thiepval Memorial (see appendix 2) at the Somme.

HINTON, HARRY JAMES 1898–1917

Private Harry James Hinton of the 2nd Battalion Dorsetshire Regiment (see appendix 1) was the younger brother of Frank Hinton (see above). Harry was born in Wimborne in February 1898, some three years later than Frank. In 1911 Harry was still at school.

The Second Battalion was deployed for the defence of the Tigris in September 1916 then, in January 1917, the battalion was transferred to the 9th Brigade of the Indian Division. It was in Iraq that Harry was killed in action on 21st March 1917, when he was just 19 years old. He is listed on the Basra Memorial (see appendix 2) in Iraq.

Frank and Harry's parents must have been devastated to lose two sons in 31 days.

HAMES, HARRY WILLIAM 1897–1917

Private Harry William Hames of the 6th Battalion Dorsetshire Regiment (see appendix 1) was a local boy through and through. He was born in Wimborne in July 1897, the fourth of five children born to Edwin and Eliza Hames. Edwin was a brickmaker and they lived in Ferndown. In 1911 they were living in Sandy Lane, Ferndown.

The 6th battalion was busy fighting various battles; the first and second of Scarpe, the Capture of Rouex, and the first and second of Passchendaele. During one of these, Harry was killed in action on 21st February 1917, aged 19. He is buried in Grove Town Cemetery, Méaulte, (see appendix 2) on the Somme.

BECKETT, GEORGE HERBERT 1896–1917

Private George Herbert Beckett, 1st/4th Battalion Hampshire Regiment (see appendix 1) was born in Sutton, Surrey in January 1896, the second of the three children of George and Mary Jane Beckett. Still living in Sutton in 1911, young George was a 'shop boy'.

On his forces record, George is shown as living in Ferndown, Dorset. By 1916, the 1st/4th Hampshires were attached to the 36th Indian Brigade of the 14th Indian Division, fighting in Mesopotamia where, on 24th February 1917, George died in action at the age of 21. His name appears on the Basra Memorial (see appendix 2) in Iraq.

MIDDLETON, HERBERT CHARLES 1893–1917

Gunner Herbert Charles Middleton of the 51st Brigade, Royal Field Artillery (see appendix 1) was a local boy, born in Longham to William John and Mary Ann Middleton, and the middle one of three children. They all lived in Ringwood Road, Longham, Dorset.

By 1911, Herbert was a Groom/Gardener. He was attached to 'C' Battery, 51st Brigade of the Royal Field Artillery. He would have been on medium-sized guns, close to the front line in France, where he was fatally wounded and, on 19th March 1917, he was to die of those wounds. He was 23. His grave is in the Faubourg-d'Amiens Cemetery (see appendix 2), at Arras, Northern France.

HOPPER, FREDERICK WALTER WILLIAM 1892–1917

Private Frederick Walter William Hopper of the 1st/1st Battalion Oxfordshire and Buckinghamshire Light Infantry (see appendix 1) was born in Wimbledon in August 1892. Frederick was one of John and Sarah Hopper's six children. In 1901, they were living in Kingston, Surrey. By 1911, Frederick was boarding in Ringwood Road, Longham and was a carter by trade. He was married in August 1915 to a Bessie Coward, and in his Forces Record, Bessie was living at 'Greenwood' in Albert Road, Ferndown.

Frederick would have been involved in the German retreat to the Hindenburg Line and the battles of Langemark and Poelcapelle. It was at this time he was seriously wounded and died on 1st April 1917 at the age of 24. He is buried in the Military Cemetery at Bray-sur-Somme (see appendix 2), in France.

WOOLRIDGE, JOHN 1884–1917

Private John Woolridge of the 9th Battalion King's Own Yorkshire Light Infantry (see appendix 1) was born in Aldershot, Hampshire in January 1884. This is according to his war record; however, I could not find him in the births section of the listings. This is not unusual. He is shown living in Okeford Fitzpaine, near Blandford in Dorset. His widow is listed as living at 111, Queen's Road, Loughborough in Leicestershire.

The 9th Battalion was very busy fighting in the Scarpe, Bullecourt and Broodseinde as well as the second battle of Passchendaele. During one of these conflicts John was killed in action and died on 9th April 1917 at the age of 33. He is buried in the Wancourt British Cemetery (see appendix 2) near Arras in Northern France.

BRADFORD, HARRY ALFRED JAMES 1893–1917

Private Harry Alfred James Bradford of the 1st Battalion Devonshire Regiment (see appendix 1) was born in Branksome, Dorset in October 1893. His father does not appear on the 1901 census, listing his mother, Mary, as a laundress. Harry had two brothers; one older, one younger. 1911 finds Harry not at home, although at 18 he may have already left. There are no records showing where he was living at this time.

Harry joined the Army on 2nd September 1914, listing his residence as 2, King's Road, Parkstone. The 1st Devonshires were spread across the European Theatre and fighting in the battle of Vimy, Scarpe, Polygon Wood, Broodseinde, Poelcapelle and the second Battle of Passchendaele. During one of these he was killed in action on 23rd April 1917 at the age of 23. His name appears on the Arras Memorial in the Faubourg-d'Amiens Cemetery (see appendix 2) in Arras, France.

SHEPHARD, FREDERICK WILLIAM 1889–1917

Private Frederick William Shephard of the 6th Battalion Dorsetshire Regiment (see appendix 1) was born in Lyme Regis, Dorset in May 1889 to Frederick and Mary Shephard, and was the eldest of their six children.

By the 1911 census he was boarding at 3, Waverley Terrace, Wimborne. Frederick married Cicely Hall in May 1913 in Ringwood, Hampshire and moved to 'The Laurels', Canford Bottom, Dorset.

As with many others in the 6th Dorsetshire, he was at various battles on the French mainland and was killed in action on 11th May 1917 aged 28. His was another name to appear on the Arras Memorial in the Faubourg-d'Amiens Cemetery (see appendix 2) in Arras, France.

GALE, WILLIAM GEORGE 1897–1917

Private William George Gale of the 1st/4th Battalion Dorsetshire Regiment (see appendix 1) was born in Parkstone, Dorset in February 1897. His parents were William and Alice Gale, and William was the eldest of five children. The Gales lived in Britannia Road, Parkstone. By 1911, they had moved to Wessex Road, Parkstone, where William was an errand boy.

The 1st/4th went to India in 1914 and, in 1916, were sent to Iraq. In 1917 they were involved in the Action of As Asilan, during which William was killed in action on 22nd May 1917 at the age of 20. His name appears on the Basra Memorial (see appendix 2). Because of the sensitivity of the area, the memorial has been moved from its original site on the west bank of the Shat-al-Arab, and is now some 15 miles further on, in the middle of what was a major battleground in the First Gulf War.

KING, LAURENCE 1898–1917

Private Laurence King of the 6th Dorsetshire Regiment (see appendix 1) was born in the local area in September 1898, the youngest of three boys raised by Samuel and Charlotte King. They lived in 'Baker Cottage' Canford Bottom. By 1911, Samuel had died and Laurence was at school.

As with other casualties of the 6th, Laurence was killed in action at the first battle of Passchendaele on 15th October 1917 at the age of just 18. He is buried in the Dozinghem Military Cemetery, Poperinghe (see appendix

2) in West Vlaanderen, Belgium. This must have been particularly hard on his widowed mother, having lost his brother Ernest (see earlier in August 1915) two years earlier.

HISCOCK, EDWARD JAMES 1888–1917

Private Edward (Ted) James Hiscock of the 9th Battalion Devonshire Regiment (see appendix 1) was born in August 1888 in Holdenhurst, Moordown, Dorset to James and Sarah Anne Hiscock, as the second of four children. They moved from Holdenhurst to Longham before 1911 by which time Ted was a young man and a bricklayer to his father by profession. He married Maggie E Ricketts from West Moors in July 1914 and their address is listed as 306, Longham, Dorset.

Ted's Devonshire regiment fought alongside the Dorsetshires in Europe. The 9th Battalion was in the second battle of Passchendaele, where Ted perished in action on 26th October 1917 aged 29. His name appears on the Tyne Cot Memorial to the Missing, near Ieper in Belgium (see appendix 2).

HART, GEORGE 1895–1917

Private George Hart of the 14th Battalion Worcestershire Regiment was born in November 1895. He was the fifth of six children born to John and Mary Hart. John was a master baker and they lived in Ringwood Road, Longham. In 1911 they were still at the same address.

George joined the Worcesters and, the 14th, also known as the Severn Valley Pioneers, served in northern France. During 1917, they fought in several battles including Scarpe, Arleux, Passchendaele, Ypres and the action of Welsh Ridge. George was fatally wounded and died on 7th November 1917. He is buried in Boulogne East Cemetery (see appendix 2) just outside Boulogne-sur-Mer on the French Coast.

HART, HARRY GEORGE 1886–1917

Private Harry George Hart of the 5th Battalion Wiltshire Regiment (see appendix 1) was born locally in May 1886. His parents were John and Mary Hart, and he was the second of six children. They all lived next door to the Infants School in Longham, Dorset. By 1901, Harry was an apprentice to a bread maker (his father was a baker's assistant). Harry was married in May 1903 to Beatrice Bessie Light in Blandford, Dorset and after Harry's death Beatrice moved to Park Street, Salisbury, Wiltshire.

The 5th Battalion was sent to Gallipoli in 1915 and fought the Turkish armies. They moved on to Mesopotamia in 1916. During 1917 this company of soldiers fought many battles including Kut al Amara, Delli Abas and Shatt al-Adhaim. During one of these, Harry was fatally wounded and died of his wounds on Christmas Day 1917. His name appears on the Kirkee Memorial (see appendix 2) near Poona in India.

The two brothers, George and Harry, died just 44 days apart. I cannot imagine the grief their parents and family must have suffered at their loss.

SHEARING, ERNEST LEWIS JOHN 1897–1917

Lance Corporal Ernest Lewis John Shearing of the 2nd/7th Battalion Hampshire Regiment (see appendix 1) was born locally in October 1897 to Arthur George and Ellen Shearing. He was their third child out of seven. They lived throughout the period in Little Canford. In 1911 Ernest is recorded as still at school.

During Ernest's service, his battalion was sent to India in 1915 and moved on to Mesopotamia in 1917. Ernest was killed in action, probably in the Battle of Tikrit, on 8th December 1917. His remains are buried in the North Baghdad Cemetery (see appendix 2).

HART, ERNEST 1886–1918

Stoker First Class Ernest Hart was born on 4th October 1886 in Hampreston, Dorset. Information is a little sketchy as to his birth as the only record I can confirm is a Royal Navy War Graves Roll which lists Ernest, and gives his parent as Mrs E Hart. The only E Hart I can find is an Ernest Hart born 2 years earlier in Warwickshire, so it is difficult to confirm this.

However, I can confirm that this particular Ernest was from Wimborne, even though I cannot find a birth record, and served on HMS *Firedrake* (not *Firebrake* as shown on the memorial) during the war. His Destroyer was  involved in the capture of German U-boat UC-5 and the destruction of UC-51 in November 1917. Ernest was subsequently struck by disease and died on 13th February 1918 at the age of 32. He is buried in the Royal Naval Cemetery in Haslar, Portsmouth (see appendix 2).

LONGMAN, VICTOR HARRY GEORGE 1891–1918

Private Victor Harry George Longman of the 2nd/1st Battalion Oxford and Buckinghamshire Light Infantry (see appendix 1) was born in Hampreston in 1891 and lived his life in 'Laurel Cottage' in Ferndown, Dorset. He was the youngest of four children born to Henry and Fanny Longman. Henry was a 'Plate Layer' on the railway (that is fish-plates which are the metal supports for the track which sit on the sleepers). By 1911, Victor had become an agricultural labourer.

The 2nd/1st Battalion disbanded in February 1918 and transferred to the 25th Entrenching Battalion with members of the Warwickshire Regiment. Their job was to maintain the trenches and back up the main force as required. Victor was killed in action on 1st April 1918, just before the battalion was disbanded. He was just 20 years old. His name appears on the Pozières Memorial (see appendix 2), which is in a small village four miles from Albert, in northern France.

BRITTEN, GILBERT SIDNEY 1895–1918

Private Gilbert Sidney Britten of the 15th Battalion Cheshire Regiment (see appendix 1) was born near Fordingbridge in Hampshire in November 1895. He was the only child of Sidney and Betty Caroline Britten. Sidney had his own farm. By 1911, Gilbert was also working on the farm. At some point after 1911, the family are listed on service records as living at 'Pennryn' on Leigh Road, Wimborne.

The 15th Battalion became involved in many battles in northern France, including, in 1917 to 1918 those of Bapaume, Ypres, Courtrai and the action of Tieghem. It was during one of the actions that Gilbert was fatally wounded and died of his injuries on 19th April 1918 at the age of 22. He is buried in the Bagneux Cemetery in Gezaincourt (see appendix 2), a village just south of Doullens.

KENT, RALPH EDWARD DAWSON 1888–1918

Lieutenant Colonel Ralph Edward Dawson Kent of the 4th Battalion of the Alexandra, Princess of Wales's Own Yorkshire Regiment (see appendix 1) was born in New Basford, Nottingham in 1888, son of Daniel L and Lucy Kent, and the youngest of four children. In 1891 we find him at a boarding school in Macclesfield, Cheshire. He was back home in 1901 and by 1911 was in the Regiment. The following account is the work of the late Robert Coulson, who has done much work on this Regiment and I am grateful to him for this information.

Lt Col RED Kent

Ralph Kent had been an Officer in the war from the start, being promoted to Acting Captain on 13th October 1914. He was Officer in Command of the 4th Yorkshire Battalion at this time. On the first day of the Battle of the Somme, on 1st July 1916, he had been in charge of 'A' Company in a battalion of the 7th Yorkshire Regiment. This unit was facing Fricourt on that day and the battalion were under orders to wait in their trenches for an attack later in the day. Devastating fire was being brought on the West Yorkshires from a machine gun post at Wing Corner and Major Kent, against orders, led 'A' Company into an assault on this position. They met intense fire and officers and men were 'mown down', resulting in over one hundred casualties and a badly wounded Major Kent and two other officers lying in front of the wire being fired on. It was only after dark that they were able to be brought in. The regimental history makes little of this episode and Major Kent seems to have avoided censure for his part.

Once recovered from his wounds, he joined the 4th Battalion in April 1918 at Bethune. By now promoted to Lieutenant Colonel, Ralph Kent was in action with the 4th at the Battle of the Lys from 9th April onwards. On 26th May 1918 they suffered an unexpectedly heavy German attack that caused heavy losses; many were killed and numerous prisoners were taken.

On the following day, Ralph was killed in action aged 29. His body was never found. He had been mentioned in despatches and was awarded the 'Croix de Guerre' by the French.

He left a widow, Alice, who lived at 'Oak Dene' Ferndown, Dorset. His name appears on the Soissons Memorial (see appendix 2) on the left bank of the River Aisne, about 60 miles north-east of Paris.

COWARD, BERTIE 1894–1918

Private Bertie Coward of the 2nd Battalion Dorsetshire Regiment (see appendix 1) was born in Hampreston in February 1894 to Albert John and Fanny Coward. Bertie was the third child of eight. Throughout his life, his family lived in Ringwood Road, Longham. By 1911 Bertie had left school and was labouring.

The Second Battalion was sent to India at the start of the war but was transferred to Egypt in 1916. Bertie was killed in action in what is now Israel on 10th August 1918 at the age of 24. He is buried in the Ramleh War Cemetery (see appendix 2) situated between Tel Aviv and Jerusalem.

BARBER, FREDERICK HENRY 1898–1918

Private Frederick Henry Barber of the 6th Battalion Dorsetshire Regiment (see appendix 1) was born in April 1898, possibly to Alfred and Louisa Barber of Burghclere, Berkshire. By 1911 he had been adopted by Frederick and Alice Hill of Wareham Road, Corfe Mullen.

The Sixth Battalion was involved throughout 1918 in many skirmishes, including the battles of Bapaume, Amiens, Albert, Havrincourt, Epehy, Cambrai, the Selle, and the Sambre. During one such battle, Frederick was killed doing his duty on 1st September 1918. He was only 19. Frederick's name appears on the Vis-en-Artois Memorial (see appendix 2), between Arras and Cambrai.

SQUIRE, WILLIAM HENRY NOEL 1899–1918

Pioneer William Henry Noel Squire of the Corps of Royal Engineers (see appendix 1) was born in Chard, Somerset. His birth was registered in January 1899, but the 'Noel' in his name suggests he could have been born on Christmas Day 1898. His parents were Wallace and Elizabeth Squire and they had six children, of which William was second eldest. They had later moved to Hampreston and Wallace was a market gardener.

The grave of William Squire in Hampreston Churchyard

From October 1916 the Royal Engineers worked underground constructing tunnels for the troops in preparation for the Battle of Arras in 1917. I cannot find how William died, but his death occurred on 1st September 1918 and he was 19. He is buried in Hampreston Churchyard (see appendix 2), very close to his family home.

MANSTON, LEONARD FREDERICK 1896–1918

Private Leonard Frederick Manston of the 8th Battalion Canadian Infantry (see appendix 1) was born in Alderholt, Dorset, to Tom and Lewina Manston on 29th June 1896. Shortly after 1911 they all moved to 4, Kinson Grove, Kinson, Dorset.

The 8th Battalion fought as part of the 2nd Infantry Brigade, 1st Canadian Division throughout 1917 and 1918. On 2nd September 1918, Leonard was killed in action in France aged 22. His name appears on the Vimy Memorial (see appendix 2), which overlooks the Douai Plain from the highest point of Vimy Ridge.

VATCHER, JAMES 1896–1918

Rifleman James Vatcher of the King's Royal Rifle Corps (see appendix 1) was born in Christchurch on the Dorset/Hampshire border in August 1896. His father and mother were James and Kate Vatcher. He was one of only two children. According to the census, by 1911 James was an apprentice brickmaker. At some point he left Christchurch and moved to Wimborne, though exactly whereabouts or when is unclear.

The Rifle Corps fought in many difficult battles throughout the war; 1918 was no different, including engagements at Estaires, Hazebrouck, Bethune, Drocourt-Quéant, St Quentin Canal, Beaurevoir, Selle and the Sambre. It was on 25th September 1918 in one of these last battles that James was killed in action at the age of 22. His body was never found and his name appears on the Memorial in Vis-en-Artois (see appendix 2), a small village between Arras and Cambrai in Northern France.

BARTLETT, EDWARD CHARLES 1895–1918

Private (Signaller) Edward Charles Bartlett of the 1st Battalion Dorsetshire Regiment (see appendix 1) was born in Ferndown, Dorset in June 1895, the son of William and Mary Bartlett, and the eldest of three children. By 1911, Edward, still living with his family in Ferndown, was listed as a labourer.

Edward joined up in August 1914 to the 3rd Dorsetshires, but was transferred to the 1st at some point, probably when the 3rd was moved to Wyke Regis. Alongside his comrades in the 1st he fought throughout the War, culminating at the Battle of Ypres and the final advance in Flanders. It was in this action that Edward was killed on 29th September 1918 at the age of 23. He is buried in the Cerisy-Gailly Military Cemetery (see appendix 2), near Albert, between Paris and Lille in north east France.

VINCENT, WILLIAM JEFFERSON 1899–1918

Second Lieutenant William Jefferson Vincent of the 1st/5th Dorsetshire Regiment (see appendix 1) was born in October 1899 in Maryport, Cumberland. He was a son of Hector and Blanche Vincent of West Moors, and the eldest of three children. In 1911 they were living in Victoria Road, Ferndown (then part of West Moors). Blanche came from the area, while Hector was a bricklayer from Northumberland. Records show William was still at school in 1911.

During the First World War, William joined the 1st Battalion, Dorsetshire Regiment and transferred later to the 5th. In 1918, the 5th was involved in the battles of the Scarpe, Drocourt-Quéant line, Canal du Nord, Cambrai and the Sambre. It was during the latter that William was killed in action on 1st October 1918 aged just 19, and very young indeed to be an Officer. He is buried in the Sucrerie Cemetery (see appendix 2), in Epinoy, a small village between Cambrai and Douai in northern France.

FLIPPANT, ALFRED SIDNEY 1891–1919

Sapper Alfred Sidney Flippant of the 10th Railway Company of the Royal Engineers (see appendix 1) was born in West Moors in August 1891 to William and Fanny Flippant, the third of four children. William was a railway labourer. Alfred was baptised on 16th August 1891 at Hampreston Church. By 1911 we find Alfred working as a nursery gardener, but he also joined up with the Royal Engineers in one of the railway companies. Alfred was married in October 1914 to Kate Green, and they lived in Station Road, West Moors.

By the end of the war the Engineers were involved in tunnelling to connect the trenches. Some of the troops were underground for months at a time. Alfred was killed in action on 1st March 1919 at the age of 29 in Belgium and he was buried in the Theux Communal Cemetery (see appendix 2) just outside Liège.

DACOMBE, PERCIVAL ALFRED 1892–1919

Driver Percival Alfred Dacombe of the Royal Army Service Corps (see appendix 1) was born in Parkstone, Dorset in February 1892 to Alfred Hubert and Elizabeth Dacombe, the second of eight surviving children from 11. They were still living in this area in 1901. By 1911 they had moved to 'Fairstowe', Victoria Road, Ferndown and Percy was an apprentice bricklayer in his father's business and renowned for having an excellent singing voice.

Percy joined up in August 1914 as a driver. Wherever transport was needed, whether it be goods or personnel, the RASC were called in to do their job. Percy survived till the end of hostilities. He and his fellow soldiers were told to make their way to the Belgian and French coasts to pick up a ship home. Percy's family received a telegram of the good news. But, it was not to be. Once in Zeebrugge, Percy contracted Spanish Flu and died within two days on 5 March 1919 aged 27. Another telegram was sent at which point his mother collapsed and died four weeks later. His father was devastated, turned to drink and within months was bankrupt. Percy is buried in the Janval Cemetery (see appendix 2) in Dieppe, Normandy.

BARRETT, GEORGE FREDERICK 1885-1919

Gunner George Frederick Barrett was born in Branksome, Bournemouth in 1885 to George Frederick and Jane Barrett, moving to Croydon in Surrey before 1901.

In 1911 we find him in barracks with the First King's Dragoon Guards. He must have switched to the Machine Gun Corps during the war. His death is recorded in France on 27th February 1919 and his burial in the Etaples Military Cemetery in Pas-de-Calais. This was well after hostilities had ended, so he died either of wounds sustained during the fighting or he contracted a disease (Spanish Flu?) in convalescence. However this George Barrett has no obvious connection to this area.

Doing my detective work studying the memorials at both Hampreston and Ferndown, the following clues are: There is no GF Barrett on the First war memorial in Hampreston, but he appears on the Ferndown one, said to be a direct copy. George appears as an addendum at the base of the Second World War memorial in Hampreston (the two memorials are separate pieces of stone), but does not appear on the Second World war listing on the Ferndown memorial. You will find George Frederick Barrett in our Second World War dead, who was in the Dorset Regiment.

I think that the name was added to the Hampreston stone after 1945 but added out of sequence. If I am wrong, then our man above must be him, with an unknown link to the area. I will leave you to decide.

Ferndown Remembrance Garden

PART TWO:

THE SECOND WORLD WAR

INTRODUCTION TO PART TWO

The casualties of the Second World War were fewer than from the First, but we are much more certain as to the accuracy of the information. However, we will not have census information for this period for another thirty of forty years, so the detail of where these people lived is much more difficult to find.

Most of the information shown is gained from Forces War Records and the Commonwealth War Graves Commission. I am also indebted to Nick Hollingworth of Hampreston for his help and advice. I have 'borrowed' one or two photos from the internet for illustration. They were not copyrighted but I hope the owners of the pictures will accept my thanks for their use.

As with the First World War casualties I have listed them in order of their death.

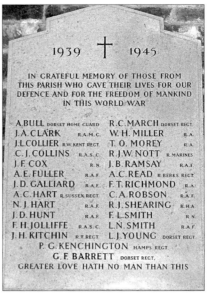

Memorial inside Hampreston
(All Saints) Church

Memorial outside The Royal British Legion, Ferndown

NOTT, RICHARD JOHN WILLIAM 1913–1940

Captain Richard John William Nott of the Royal Marines (see appendix 1) was born and grew up in Wimborne. He was the son of Gilbert Harwood Nott and Grace Emily Nott.

Aircraft Carrier HMS Glorious

Richard had joined HMS *Glorious*, one of the Royal Navy's Aircraft Carriers and was onboard on the morning of 8th June 1940 when, together with the destroyers HMS *Acasta* and HMS *Ardent*, they were intercepted by the German Battle Cruisers *Gneisenau* and *Scharnhorst*. This took place in the Norwegian Sea. The three ships were sunk by gunfire in a little over two hours with the loss of over 1,500 officers and men of the Navy, Marines and Air Force. There were only 39 survivors. Many questions remain unanswered about the attack, and why more action did not happen. Books have been written about the incident. Richard lost his life that day at the age of 27. His name appears on the Lee-on-Solent Memorial.

RAMSAY, JOHN BASIL 1919–1940

Pilot Officer John Basil Ramsay has not proved to have a reliable birth record, but he was born in 1919. His family lived in Lilliput, Dorset. He was the son of Allan and Esme Sarah Ramsay.

John was in 151 Squadron of the Royal Air Force (see appendix 1) stationed at North Weald Airfield near Epping, north east of London. While flying a Hawker Hurricane, he apparently crashed near Burnham-on-Crouch in Essex on 18th August 1940 and is listed as killed in action at the age of 21. Like many pilots, he is buried in the Brookwood Military Cemetery near Pirbright in Surrey, the largest war cemetery in Britain.

Hawker Hurricane

COX, JAMES FRANK 1900–1940

Leading Seaman James Frank Cox, Royal Navy (see appendix 1) was born in Paddington, London in November 1900 to Frank and Georgina Cox. In 1901 they were living in Wilmington, Kent, with James as their only son. By 1911 we find them in Stapehill, by which time Frank is a garden labourer and there are four more children, one only a few days old. James married Annie Laura Louise King in Hampreston Church on 22nd November 1925.

James went to sea with the Navy and joined HM Submarine *Swordfish*, an 'S' class submarine. The sub went out on patrol on 7th November 1940 to relieve HMS *Usk*, which was on patrol off the Western Approaches near Brest, France. She was never heard from again.

HM Submarine Swordfish (61S)

It was generally thought she had been sunk by a German destroyer; however, in 1983, about 12 miles off St Catherine's Point on the Isle of Wight, a local diver found the sub and reported that she was split just forward of the gun turret. It was clear that she had struck a mine and sunk. The submarine has since been designated a 'protected wreck site'.

HUNT, JAMES DOUGLAS 1911–1940

Sergeant James Douglas Hunt of 83 Squadron RAF (see appendix 1) was born in 1921 to James John and Florence Hunt of Ferndown, Dorset. No 83 Squadron was based at Scampton Air Base, now the base for the famous Red Arrows.

Handley Page Hampden bomber

James and his squadron were in action from the first day of the war, carrying out sweeps of the North Sea looking for German warships. Bombing missions started in April 1940, using Handley Page Hampden bombers. It was two years later that they changed to Lancasters. James was killed in action on 28th December 1940. He was only 19. He is buried in Benson (St Helen) churchyard in Oxfordshire. Benson and the next village, Chalgrove, are well known as airfields. Benson is still operational and now flies helicopters, while Chalgrove was a base for photo-reconnaissance aircraft during the war.

BULL, ALFRED 1884–1941

Alfred Bull was a volunteer in the Dorset Home Guard. He was born locally in 1884. He married Eveline early in the 20th century.

Alfred died on 17th August 1941 and was lain to rest in Hampreston (All Saints) Churchyard. His wife died 20 years later on 23rd August 1961 aged 79, and she is buried alongside her husband.

Gravestone of Alfred and Eveline Bull

KITCHIN, JOHN HENRY 1916–1942

Captain John Henry Kitchin of the Royal Tank Regiment (see appendix 1) was born in April 1916 in Barrow-in-Furness, Lancashire to James and Margaret Joanna Kitchin (née Hooley). They had married in Ashton-under-Lyne, Lancashire in February 1912. John married Edith M Lawrence in October 1941.

Sherman tank of the 23rd Armoured Brigade

John was with the 23rd Armoured Brigade in North Africa under the command of Lieutenant Colonel JL Finigan. They fought at El Alamein. The division was sent to the Middle East in May 1942 to join the 8th Army. In mid-July 1942 the brigade was detached from the 8th Armoured Division and with the addition of the 5th Regiment of the Royal Horse Artillery became the 23rd Amoured Brigade Group. After only 14 days, the Brigade was chosen to reinforce the 30th Corps attack at the Battle of Ruweisat Ridge, during which nearly half of the tank crews were either killed or injured. They rebuilt using the 24th Armoured Brigade. In September 1942 they fought the Battle of Alam el Halfa, during which John was killed in action on 1st September at the age of 26. He is buried in the El Alamein War Cemetery in Alamein – about 80 miles west of Alexandria.

HART, ARTHUR GEORGE 1916–1942

Lance Corporal Arthur George Hart of 5th Battalion Royal Sussex Regiment (see appendix 1) was born locally to Frederick William and Louisa Hart. Arthur was to later marry Joan Ellen and they lived in Ringwood.

Arthur would have started his war in France and been involved in the battles and retreat to Dunkirk. Later, in 1942 he was sent to North Africa, still with the same brigade (133rd Royal Sussex). From August to October they were involved in the action at the Battle of Alam el Halfa, during which Arthur was killed on 27 October 1942 at the age of 26. His name appears on the Alamein Memorial within the cemetery there.

BARRETT, GEORGE FREDERICK 1905–1942

Sergeant George Frederick Barrett of the 6th Battalion Dorsetshire Regiment (see appendix 1) was born in Christchurch on the Hampshire/Dorset border in May 1905. His parents were George Frederick and Eliza Barrett. As far as I can tell, father George had been in the Dragoon Guards and had been born in Wimborne. Son George married Alice Downton in February 1925 in Poole, Dorset.

There is much less information on the campaigns in the Second World War so although we know he died on 12th November 1942, we do not know where or how. It may have been in Europe or North Africa, so far I have been unable to clarify this. George is buried in Hampreston Churchyard.

The gravestone of GF Barrett

JOLLIFFE, FREDERICK HENRY 1910–1943

Driver Frederick Henry Jolliffe of the Royal Army Service Corps (see appendix 1) was born in July 1910 in Wimborne, Dorset to Arthur and Agnes Jolliffe. He was the youngest of eight children. They lived in West Parley, where Arthur was a farm bailiff. Frederick married his wife-to-be Maureen locally.

With Frederick serving in the RASC he would have one of two roles. Either in supply, which would be supplying food, fuel, hospital and other supplies; or in transport, which would include the shipment of ammunition, engineering stores, ordnance and post from the railhead (if there was one) to the field force. I am unsure as to where Frederick died, but it was on 27th March 1943 at the age of 32 and his body was never found. His name appears on the Brookwood Memorial within the Brookwood Military Cemetery in Surrey.

KENCHINGTON, PERCY GEORGE 1906–1943

Private Percy George Kenchington of the 2nd Battalion Royal Hampshire Regiment (see appendix 1) was born in May 1906 in Fordingbridge, Hampshire to Levi Harry and Matilda M Kenchington. They were still in this area in 1911 when Percy was the eldest of four children. Their move to Ferndown would have been after this, but Percy married Jessie Matilda Wyatt in Bournemouth in November 1926.

The Second Battalion that Percy served with was sent to Africa, setting sail on 11th November 1942, to take part in 'Operation Torch'. They landed in Algiers on 21st November 1942. On 1st December 1942 the battalion came under heavy attack from a force four times their size and was forced to retreat to Tebourba. It was during this period that Percy was killed in action on 9th April 1943 at the age of 36. He is buried in El Alia Cemetery, which is 10 miles south east of Algiers, within a large civilian cemetery.

YOUNG, LESLIE JOHN 1918–1943

Sergeant Leslie John Young of the 1st Battalion, Dorsetshire Regiment (see appendix 1) was born in Christchurch in August 1918. He lived in Longham with his foster parents.

The First Battalion had been fighting in Africa and moved over to Sicily and Italy in 1943. Leslie was killed in action on 1st August 1943 at the age of 25. He is buried in the Catania War Cemetery, which is 5 miles from the town of Catania in Sicily.

FULLER, ALFRED ERIC 1923–1943

Flight Sergeant Alfred Eric Fuller of 461 Squadron Royal Air Force (see appendix 1) was born in 1923 to Alfred and Florence Fuller of Longham, Dorset.

The Short Sunderland Mk. III

Alfred's Squadron was based in Hamworthy in Poole Harbour from 1942 to 1943, then moved to Pembroke Dock in the far west of Wales. The Squadron flew Short Sunderlands, which were flying boats. During 1943 they conducted daylight anti-submarine patrols in the Bay of Biscay, where they were regularly attacked by German fighters. During 1943 the Squadron sank 3 U-boats. In May 1943, the Squadron was re-equipped with the Sunderland Mk III; a much more advanced aircraft that enabled them to operate at night. It was during one of these patrols that on 13th August 1943, Alfred was killed in action at the age of just 20. He had been awarded the Distinguished Flying Cross: 'To recognise valour, courage or devotion to duty performed whilst flying in active operations against the enemy'.

CLARK, JAMES ALFRED 1917–1943

Private James Alfred Clark, of the 157th Field Ambulance, Royal Army Medical Corps (see appendix 1) was born in London in December 1917 to James Alfred and Muriel Clark. He was married to Rose Perrin Clark. They lived in Ealing, West London. I have not found a connection to this local area, but this is the man.

The Royal Army Medical Corps is a specialist Corps engaged to provide medical services to Army personnel. The records say that James died 'at sea' on 7th August 1943, aged 25, but I cannot find any detail of where, how or why. Because his body was never recovered, his name appears on the Brookwood Memorial, near Pirbright, Surrey.

HART, NORMAN JOHN 1921–1943

Sergeant Norman John Hart of the Royal Air Force Voluntary Reserve (see appendix 1) was born locally in February 1921 to Bernard James and Elizabeth Maud Mary Hart (née Stroud). In 1911, Bernard and Elizabeth were married and living in London, but by the war they were living in Longham.

Norman joined the RAFVR and became a Flight Engineer. I cannot find details of his death other than that it was on 19th August 1943 when he was aged 22. He is buried in Hampreston (All Saints) Churchyard.

The gravestone of Norman John Hart

COLLIER, JOHN LAURENCE 1917–1943

Second Lieutenant John Laurence Collier was born in Lewisham, London to Clarence E and Margaret Collier (née Matthews) in May 1917. According to war records they lived in Folkestone, Kent but the same record states that John lived in Dorset.

John joined the Queen's Own Royal West Surrey Regiment (the oldest infantry regiment in England) (see appendix 1) but was seconded to the 4th Battalion of the Royal West Kent Regiment (see appendix 1) who were known as 'The Buffs'.

The records also state that John died 'at sea', but I have no further details. The 4th Battalion fought in the Dodecanese Campaign in the Battle of Leros, which started on 15th September 1943 and ended on 16th November that year. John died on 23rd October 1943 at the age of 26. His name appears on the Athens Memorial that stands just south east of Athens, Greece.

READ, AUBREY CHARLES GEORGE 1907–1944

Private Aubrey Charles George Read of the 10th Battalion Princess Charlotte of Wales Royal Berkshire Regiment (see appendix 1) was born in May 1907 in Wimborne to Charles George and Lily Grace Read. Aubrey was the middle offspring of three children. His father, Charles, was a carpenter. They lived at 'Glenmoor', Albert Road, Ferndown. Aubrey wed Josephine Madge King in November 1936.

With the 10th Battalion, Aubrey served in North Africa, the Middle East, Sicily and Italy as part of the 168th London Infantry Brigade. The 10th Battalion was reduced to just 40 men defending the Anzio Beachhead. In the battle around Carroceto and Aprilia, Aubrey was killed in action on 8th February 1944 at the age of 36. He is buried in the Anzio War Cemetery in Italy.

MOREY, THOMAS OWEN 1911–1944

Lance Bombardier Thomas Owen Morey was born in December 1911 in Weymouth, Dorset to Mr and Mrs George Morey. Thomas married Dorothy Steel in May 1939 and they moved to Ferndown.

Thomas joined the Royal Artillery (see appendix 1) in the 169 Battery Light Anti-Aircraft Regiment. During the war they went to Africa in 1942, fighting at El Alamein, then to Sicily in 1943 and into Italy from then on, all as part of the Eighth Army. In February 1944 the Battle of Monte Cassino took place, which involved 20 divisions attacking along a 20-mile front and eventually driving the enemy

Anti-aircraft gun of the type used by Thomas Morey

back, but at enormous cost in men. Among those who died was Thomas Morey, on 19th February 1944, at the age of 32. He is buried in the Cassino War Cemetery in Italy along with 4,270 others.

RICHMOND, FREDERICK TOM 1908–1944

Bombardier Frederick Tom Richmond of 109 Light Anti-Aircraft Anti-Tank Regiment Royal Artillery (see appendix 1) was born in Wimborne, in September 1908, the son of Charles and Rose Alice Richmond. The family lived in Stapehill, although in 1911 they were living in Holt, near Wimborne. Frederick was married to Lily Elizabeth.

Frederick was serving in Nigeria, where there was an uprising as the Nigerians had started to demand independence. Sadly, on 29th February 1944, Frederick was killed in action and was interred in the Ibadan Military Cemetery. Over 130 serving soldiers are buried there.

SMITH, FRANK LEONARD C1924–1944

Frank Leonard Smith is listed on the RBL Ferndown memorial as being in the Royal Navy (see appendix 1). The closest one I can find in the records is Able Seaman Frank Leonard Smith who served on HMS *Asphodel*. This Frank was the son of Arthur and ESH Smith of Manor Park, Essex. I cannot find a connection with this area. If anyone can shed light on this, please let me know.

HMS Asphodel (K56),
a Flower class Corvette

The record indicates that Frank died on 9th March 1944. The history of the ship shows that it was sunk by a torpedo fired from U-575 *Boehmer* at 01.54 on 10th March 1944, during an attack on convoy SL-150. This all took place in the Bay of Biscay. There were only five survivors from a crew of 97. Frank was only 20 years old. His name appears on the Chatham Naval Memorial in Kent.

MILLER, WILLIAM HARRY 1905–1944

Gunner William Harry Miller of the Royal Artillery (see appendix 1) was born in Winchester, Hampshire in January 1905, son of John Andrew and Emily Miller. By 1911, John had died but Emily was still living in the same place with seven children of which William was the fifth. William married Louie some time before the outbreak of war, possibly in October 1928. The service record only identifies his wife's name, but the marriage records show only two William H Millers, neither of whom married a 'Louie'. In October 1928, though, a marriage took place in Bournemouth of William H Miller and Cecilia E Tomes. I think it likely that this was our William.

The 23rd Field Regiment of the Royal Artillery was based in Exeter and went to France in 1939. They were transferred to Tunisia in 1941 and fought through the Middle East heading to Salerno, Italy by September 1943. They fought through Italy during 1944. In June 1944 they met the retreating German 14th Army, who entrenched at Bolsena (about 80 miles north of Rome) and a tank battle ensued against the German Panzer tanks. There were many casualties and William became one of them on 1st July 1944 at the age of 40. He is buried in the Bolsena War Cemetery.

COLLINS, CLIFFORD JOHN 1920–1944

Driver Clifford John Collins of the Royal Army Service Corps (see appendix 1) was born in Swindon in May 1920 to Joseph Thomas and Rose Cecil Collins. Clifford married Doris Elizabeth and they lived in Ferndown.

As a driver, Clifford would be required to transport goods, ammunition and people to wherever they were needed. By the end of 1944, the allies were working their way north through Italy and, by November 1944, had reached what is known as the 'Gothic' line in the Apennine Mountains. During the advance from Rimini to Forli between September and November, the weather was atrocious – flooding river after river and hampering the advancing troops. Clifford was killed on 23rd November 1944 at the age of 24. He is buried alongside 774 other casualties of this period in the Cesena War Cemetery near Rimini in north-east Italy.

GALLIARD, JOHN DOUGLAS 1921–1944

I can find no birth records for John; however, there is a record which suggests he was born in Germany (no date) which I think is reliable. There is no record of his getting married or living locally. However, as he is on our memorial, we presume he did.

Flight Sergeant John Douglas Galliard was a wireless operator/air gunner with the Royal Air Force Volunteer Reserve (see appendix 1) attached to 619 Squadron. This Squadron (known as the 'Forgotten' Squadron) was based at RAF Strubby in Lincolnshire by 1944. On 4th December 1944 the Squadron was part of a raid over Germany and John's Lancaster,

LM751 was shot down over Freudenstadt. There was one survivor who became a POW. I am grateful to Shaun McGuire for this information and the photograph of the crew.

The crew of ND932, PG–U were:

FO Stanley Victor Chambers, RCAF, killed
Sgt Archie Pascoe, RAFVR, killed
Sgt Charles John Reed, RAFVR, killed
PO Ira Walter Shantz, RCAF, killed
F/Sgt John Douglas Galliard, RAFVR, killed
F/Sgt Robert Prunkle, RCAF, killed
F/Sgt G H Goudy, RCAF, prisoner of war

ROBSON, CLIFFORD ALLAN 1921–1945

Flying Officer Clifford Allan Robson of 156 Squadron Royal Air Force Volunteer Reserve (see appendix 1) was born in Wiltshire in June 1921. His parents were Allan and Florence Blanche Robson and they lived in Ferndown.

Clifford's 156 Squadron was a heavy bomber group based at RAF Upwood in Cambridgeshire flying Lancasters. Clifford was killed on his first training mission on 11th March 1945. He is buried in Hampreston (All Saints) Churchyard.

Gravestone of Clifford Allan Robson

SHEARING, ROBERT JAMES 1914–1945

A personal history for Gunner Robert James Shearing of the 3rd Regiment Royal Horse Artillery (see appendix 1) is somewhat elusive. The only record I can find for Robert is his birth in September 1914 in Wimborne. His mother's maiden name was Maidment. There is a record of a marriage between Arthur G Shearing and Maud Maidment in 1917 in Poole, Dorset, which seems a likely match.

The Third Regiment was part of the 7th Armoured Division operating in northern Europe in 1945 and fighting towards the end of the war. Somewhere near the Dutch border with Germany, Robert was killed in the line of duty on 4th April 1945 at the age of 30. He is buried in the Reichswald Forest War Cemetery in the Town of Kleve.

SMITH, LESLIE NORMAN 1923–1945

Flight Sergeant Leslie Norman Smith of the Royal Air Force Volunteer Reserve (see appendix 1) was born in December 1923 in Wimborne. His father was Frederick James Smith. I cannot find a marriage record but they lived in the local area.

Sadly, I cannot find any detail of Leslie Smith's service other than the date of his death, which was 28th August 1945. Clearly this was after the war was finished, so it is even more mysterious. Also, his grave is not a designated war grave.

MARCH, RC

Here we have a real issue. The Ferndown memorial says that this gentleman served in the Dorset Regiment. There is no RC March listed in any service in World War II. I have tried alternative spellings but still no one has surfaced. Mr March is a mystery! If you have any ideas or clues as to this man's identity I would love to hear from you.

As we leave this section on our war dead from the First and Second World Wars, I am reminded of this poem:

In Flanders Fields

In Flanders fields the poppies blow
Between the crosses, row on row,
That mark our place; and in the sky
The larks, still bravely singing, fly
Scarce heard amid the guns below.

We are the dead. Short days ago
We lived, felt dawn, saw sunset glow,
Loved and were loved, and now we lie
In Flanders fields.

Take up our quarrel with the foe:
To you from failing hands we throw
The torch; be yours to hold it high.
If ye break faith with us who die
We shall not sleep, though poppies grow
In Flanders fields.

Lieutenant Colonel John McCrae, MD (1872–1918) of the Canadian Army wrote this poem in May 1915, after the Second Battle of Ypres. It is incredibly moving; I think you will agree.

APPENDIX 1

REGIMENTS FROM THE WAR MEMORIAL

WORLD WAR I

Argyll & Sutherland Highlanders during World War I

The regiment raised a total of 16 battalions and was awarded 68 battle honours, 6 Victoria Crosses and lost 6,900 men during the course of the First World War.

1st Battalion

04.08.1914 – Stationed at Dinapore, India.

19.10.1914 – Embarked for England from Bombay, arriving at Plymouth 19.11.1914 and then moved to Winchester to join the 81st Brigade of the 27th Division.

20.12.1914 – Mobilised for war and landed at Le Havre, then engaged in various actions on the Western Front including:

1915 – The action of St Eloi, The Second Battle of Ypres.

27.11.1915 – Embarked for Macedonia from Marseilles, arriving at Salonika 12.12.1915, engaged in various actions against the Bulgarian Army including:

1916 – The capture of Karajakois, The capture of Yenikoi, The battle of Tumbitza Farm.

1917 – The capture of Homondos.

1918 – The capture of the Roche Noir Salient, the passage of the Vardar River and the pursuit to the Strumica valley.

30.09.1918 – Ended the war at Izlis, north-west of Doiran, Macedonia.

Oxford and Buckinghamshire Light Infantry during World War I

The regiment raised 18 battalions and was awarded 59 battle honours and 2 Victoria Crosses. They lost 5,880 men during the course of the First World War.

1/1st Buckinghamshire Battalion Territorial Force

04.08.1914 – Stationed at Aylesbury as part of the South Midland Brigade of the South Midland Division, then moved to Writtle near Chelmsford.

30.03.1915 – Mobilised for war and landed at Boulogne, France.

May 1915 – The formation became the 145th Brigade of the 48th Division, which engaged in various actions on the Western Front including:

1916 – The Battle of Albert, The Battle of Bazentin Ridge, The Battle of Pozières Ridge, The Battle of the Ancre Heights, The Battle of the Ancre.

1917 – The German Retreat to the Hindenburg Line, The Battle of Langemarck, The Battle of Polygon Wood, The Battle of Broodseinde, The Battle of Poelcapelle.

Nov 1917 – Deployed to Italy to stiffen Italian resistance to enemy attack following a disaster at Caporetto.

1918 – The Division held the front line sector at Montello and then moved west to the Asiago sector and then engaged in fighting on the Asiago Plateau, The Battle of the Vittoria Veneto in Val d'Assa.

04.11.1918 – Ended the war near Trent, Austria.

2/1st Buckinghamshire Battalion Territorial Force

Sep 1914 – Formed at Aylesbury.

Jun 1915 – Moved to Northampton and joined the 184th Brigade of the 61st Division and then moved to Chelmsford.

Mar 1916 – Moved to Salisbury Plain.

26.05.1916 – Mobilised for war and landed at Le Havre and engaged in various actions on the Western Front including:

1916 – The Attack at Fromelles (unsuccessful diversionary tactic during the Battle of the Somme).

1917 – The Operations on the Ancre, the German retreat to the Hindenburg Line, the Battle of Langemarck, the German counter attacks.

22.02.1918 – Disbanded at Germaine, with remaining personnel transferred to the 25th Entrenching Battalion.

Cheshire Regiment during World War I

The regiment raised 38 battalions and awarded 75 battle honours and 2 Victoria Crosses. A total of 8,413 men were lost during the course of the First World War.

1st Battalion

04.08.1914 – Stationed at Londonderry as part of the 15th Brigade of the 5th Division.

16.08.1914 – Mobilised for war, landed at Le Havre and engaged in various actions on the Western Front including:

1914 – The Battle of Mons and subsequent retreat, the Battle of Le Cateau and the Affair of Crepy-en-Valois, the Battle of the Marne, the Battle of the Aisne, the Battles of La Bassée and Messines 1914, The First Battle of Ypres.

1915 – The Second Battle of Ypres and the Capture of Hill 60.

1916 – The Attacks on High Wood, the Battle of Guillemont, the Battle of Flers-Courcelette, the Battle of Morval, the Battle of Le Transloy.

1917 – The Battle of Vimy, the Attack on La Coulotte, the Third Battle of the Scarpe, the Capture of Oppy Wood, the Battle of Polygon Wood, the Battle of Broodseinde, the Battle of Poelcapelle, the Second Battle of Passchendaele.

Dec 1917 – Deployed to Italy to strengthen Italian resistance after the disaster at the Battle of Caporetto and the Division positioned along the River Piave.

Apr 1918 – Returned to France:

The Battle of Hazebrouck, Defence of Nieppe Forest, the Battle of Albert, the Battle of Bapaume, the Battle of Drocourt-Quéant, the Battle of the Epehy, the Battle of the Canal du Nord, the pursuit to the Selle, the Battle of the Selle.

11.11.1918 – Ended the war near Le Quesnoy, France.

15th (Service) Battalion (1st Birkenhead) and 16th (Service) Battalion (2nd Birkenhead)

18.11.1914 – The 15th was formed, and on 03.12.1914 the 16th was formed, both by Alfred Bigland, MP at Birkenhead, as a Bantam Battalion and then moved to Hoylake.

Jun 1915 – Moved to Masham, Yorkshire as part of the 105th Brigade of the 35th Division and then moved to Salisbury Plain and were taken over by the War Office.

Jan 1916 – Mobilised for war by landing in Le Havre and engaging in a number of actions on the Western Front including:

1916 – The Battle of Bazentin Ridge, the fighting for Arrow Head Copse and Maltz Horn Farm, and the fighting for Falfemont Farm.

1917 – The pursuit of the German retreat to the Hindenburg Line, the fighting in Houthulst Forest, the Second Battle of Passchendaele.

1918 – The First Battle of Bapaume, the Battle of Ypres, the Battle of Courtrai, the Action of Tieghem.

11.11.1918 – Ended the war at Audenhove, north east of Renaix, Belgium.

Devonshire Regiment during World War I

The regiment raised a total of 25 battalions and fought on the Western Front; in Italy at the battles of the Piave and Vittorio Veneto; in Macedonia; Egypt; Palestine; and Mesopotamia. The regiment received 65 battle honours and two Victoria Crosses during the course of the war.

1st Battalion

04.08.1914 – Stationed in Jersey at the outbreak of war.

21.08.1914 – Mobilised for war and landed at Le Havre.

14.09.1914 – Joined the 8th Brigade of the 3rd Division.

30.09.1914 – Transferred to the 14th Brigade of the 5th Division and engaged in various actions on the Western Front including:

Autumn 1914 – The Battle of La Bassée, the Battle of Messines, the First Battle of Ypres.

Dec 1914 – This Battalion took part in the Christmas truce of 1914.

1915 – The Second Battle of Ypres and the Capture of Hill 60.

12.01.1916 – Transferred to the 95th Brigade of the 5th Division.

1916 – The Attacks on High Wood, the Battle of Guillemont, the Battle of Flers-Courcelette, the Battle of Morval, the Battle of Le Transloy.

1917 – The Battle of Vimy, the Attack on La Coulotte, the Third Battle of the Scarpe, the Battle of Polygon Wood, the Battle of Broodseinde, the Battle of Poelcapelle, the Second Battle of Passchendaele.

27.11.1917 – Moved to Italy to strengthen the Italian resistance.

07.04.1918 – Returned to France and once again engaged in various actions on the Western Front including:

During 1918 – The Battle of Hazebrouck, the Battle of Albert, the Battle of Bapaume, the Battle of Drocourt-Quéant, the Battle of the Epehy, the Battle of the Canal du Nord, the pursuit to the Selle, the Battle of the Selle.

11.11.1918 – Ended the war in France at Le Quesnoy.

9th (Service) Battalion

15.09.1914 – Formed at Exeter as part of the Second New Army (K2) and then moved to Rushmoor Camp, Aldershot, Hants as part of the 20th Division.

Oct 1914 – Moved to Bisley, then Tournai Barracks, Aldershot, and then Haslemere and finally Bordon, where they ceased to be part of the 20th Division?

28.07.1915 – Mobilised for war and landed at Le Havre and transferred to the 20th Brigade of the 7th Division, which engaged in various actions on the Western Front including

the Battle of Loos 1915.

1916 – The Battle of Albert, the Battle of Bazentin and the attacks on High Wood, the Battle of Delville Wood, the Battle of Guillemont, and operations on the Ancre.

1917 – The German retreat to the Hindenburg Line, the Arras offensive, the Battle of Polygon Wood, the Battle of Broodseinde, the Battle of Poelcapelle, the Second Battle of Passchendaele.

Nov 1917 – Moved to Italy, arriving at Legnago to strengthen the Italian resistance against the Austro-Hungarian forces and engaged in various actions including:

Dec 1917–early 1918 – The crossing the Piave and the Battle of Vittoria Veneto.

Sept 1918 – Moved to France leaving the 7th Division, arriving at St Riquier and joining the 7th Brigade of the 25th Division. Once again fighting on the Western Front including: at the Battle of Beaurevoir, the Battle of Cambrai 1918, the Pursuit to and Battle of the Selle, the Battle of the Sambre.

11.11.1918 – Ended the war in France at Landrecies.

Dorsetshire Regiment during World War I

The regiment raised a total of 12 battalions and received 57 battle honours, having lost 4,060 men during the course of the war.

1st Battalion

04.08.1914 – Stationed at Belfast as part of the 15th Brigade of the 5th Division.

16.08.1914 – Were mobilised for war, landed at Le Havre and engaged in various actions on the Western Front including:

1914 – The Battle of Mons and subsequent retreat, the Battle of Le Cateau and the Affair of Crepy-en-Valois, the Battle of the Marne, the Battle of the Aisne, the Battles of La Bassée and Messines 1914, the First Battle of Ypres.

1915 – The Second Battle of Ypres and the Capture of Hill 60.

31.12.1915 – Transferred to the 95th Brigade of the 32nd Division.

07.01.1916 – The 95th Brigade became the 14th of the same Division.

1916 – The Battle of Delville Wood, the Battle of Flers-Courcelette.

1917 – The German retreat to the Hindenburg Line, the First Battle of the Scarpe, the Third Battle of the Scarpe, the Battle of Langemarck, the First Battle of Passchendaele, the Second Battle of Passchendaele.

1918 – The Battle of St Quentin, the Battle of the Avre, the Battle of Ypres 1918 and the final advance in Flanders.

11.11.1918 – Ended the war in Flaumont, east of Avesnes, France.

2nd Battalion

04.08.1914 – Stationed at Poona, India as part of the 16th Brigade of the Poona Division.

06.11.1914 – Deployed to the Persian Gulf and landed at Fao.

29.04.1916 – 350 men captured at Kut al Amara by the Turkish Army (only 70 survived their captivity).

04.02.1916 – Composite Battalion was formed at El Orah, Tigris while battalion was besieged, from drafts and recovered wounded of the 2nd Norfolk and 2nd Dorset battalions. They were nicknamed the Norsets and became part of the 21st Brigade of the 7th Indian Division.

21.07.1916 – The Composite Battalion was broken up and the 2nd Battalion reconstituted to become the Corps Troops of the Tigris Corps.

Sep 1916 – Deployed on the Tigris Defences.

Jan 1917 – Transferred to the 9th Brigade of the 3rd Indian Division.

Apr 1918 – Deployed to Egypt, landing at Suez.

31.10.1918 – Ended the war at Zawata, south west of Nazareth, Palestine.

1/4th Battalion Territorial Force

04.08.1914 – Stationed at Dorchester as part of the South Western Brigade of the Wessex Division and then moved to Salisbury Plain.

09.10.1914 – Embarked for India at Southampton, landing at Bombay and then the Division was broken up.

18.02.1916 – Embarked for Basra from Karachi.

23.02.1916 – Transferred to the 42nd Brigade.

May 1916 – The 42nd transferred to the 15th Indian Division and engaged in various actions including:

1916 – Action of As Sahilan.

1917 – Capture of Ramadi.

1918 – Occupation of Hit and Action of Khan Baghdadi.

31.10.1918 – Ended the war near Khan Baghdadi on Euphrates, north west of Baghdad, Mesopotamia.

5th (Service) Battalion

Aug 1914 – Formed at Dorchester as part of the First New Army (K1) and then moved to Belton Park, Grantham and attached to the 11th Division.

18.01.1915 – Joined the 34th Brigade of the 11th Division.

03.07.1915 – Embarked for Gallipoli from Liverpool via Mudros and Imbros.

06.08.1915 – Landed at Suvla Bay and engaged in various actions against the Turkish Army including the Battle of Sari Bair.

16.12.1915 – Evacuated from Gallipoli to Mudros and Imbros, due to severe casualties from combat, disease and harsh weather.

01.02.1916 – Deployed to Alexandria, and took over a section of the Suez Canal defences.

03.07.1916 – Embarked for France from Alexandria, arriving at Marseilles and engaging in a number of actions on the Western Front including:

1916 – The capture of the Wundt-Werk, the Battle of Flers-Courcelette and the Battle of Thiepval.

1917 – Operations on the Ancre, the Battle of Messines, the Battle of Langemarck, the Battle of Polygon Wood, the Battle of Broodseinde and the Battle of Poelcapelle.

1918 – The Battle of the Scarpe, the Battle of the Drocourt-Quéant Line, the Battle of the Canal du Nord, the Battle of Cambrai 1918, the pursuit to the Selle, the Battle of the Sambre.

11.11.1918 – Ended the war at Les Trieux, west of Aulnois, Belgium.

6th (Service) Battalion

06.09.1914 – Formed at Dorchester as part of the Second New Army (K2) and then moved to Wareham, Dorset, attached to the 17th Division.

Mar 1915 – Transferred to the 50th Brigade of the 17th Division and then moved to Romsey, Hampshire.

14.07.1915 – Mobilised for war and landed at Boulogne. Engaged in various actions on the Western Front including:

1915 – Holding front lines in southern area of Ypres Salient.

1916 – The Battle of Albert, the Battle of Delville Wood.

1917 – The First Battle of the Scarpe, the Second Battle of the Scarpe, the Capture of Roeux, the First Battle of Passchendaele, the Second Battle of Passchendaele.

1918 – The Battle of St Quentin, the Battle of Bapaume, the Battle of Amiens, the Battle of Albert, the Battle of Havrincourt, the Battle of Epehy, the Battle of Cambrai 1918, the pursuit to the Selle, the Battle of the Selle, the Battle of the Sambre.

11.11.1918 – Ended the war at Eclaibes, north of Avesnes, France.

7th (Reserve) Battalion

Nov 1914 – Formed at Weymouth as a service battalion of the Fourth New Army (K4), forming part of the 102nd Brigade of the 34th Division.

10.04.1915 – Became a 2nd Reserve Brigade and moved to Wool and Wareham, Dorset.

Oct 1915 – Returned to Wool and joined the 8th Reserve Brigade.

01.09.1916 – Became the 35th Training Reserve Battalion.

Royal Dublin Fusiliers

The two regiments had been fighting in India in the late 18th century and were incorporated into the British Army as the 103rd Regiment of Foot (Royal Bombay Fusiliers) and 102nd Regiment of Foot (Royal Madras Fusiliers).

Both Regiments were merged in 1881 as part of the Childers Reforms, which restructured the British army infantry into a network of multi-battalion regiments of two regular and two militia battalions. They became the Royal Dublin Fusiliers. The newly formed regiment went on to serve during the Boer War (1899–1902), fighting at the siege of Ladysmith and the battles at Colenso and Tugela Heights as well as in two world wars. Three battalions of the regiment were also involved during the 1916 Easter Rising.

The regiment was disbanded in 1922, once the Irish Free State was established following the Irish War of Independence (1919–1922), along with all five British regiments recruited from the Irish Free States.

Royal Hampshire Regiment during World War I

The Regiment formed a total of 32 battalions and received 82 battle honours and 3 Victoria Crosses while losing 7,580 men during the course of the war.

2nd Battalion

04.08.1914 – Stationed at Mhow, India at the outbreak of war.

16.11.1914 – Embarked for England from Bombay, arriving at Plymouth on 22.12.1914 and then moved to Romsey.

13.02.1915 – Moved to Stratford-on-Avon and joined the 88th Brigade of the 29th Division and then moved on to Warwick.

29.03.1915 – Mobilised for war and embarked for Gallipoli from Avonmouth via Alexandria.

25.04.1915 – Landed at Gallipoli and engaged in actions including the battles for Krithia and the Achi Baba Heights.

08.01.1916 – Evacuated to Alexandria due to heavy casualties from combat, disease and severe weather conditions.

Mar 1916 – Moved to France, landing at Marseilles where the Division engaged in fighting on the Western Front including:

1916 – The Battle of Albert, the Battle of the Transloy Ridges.

1917 – The First, Second, and Third Battles of the Scarpe, the Battle of Langemarck, the Battle of Broodseinde, the Battle of Poelcapelle and the Battle of Cambrai.

During 1918 – The Battle of Estaires, the Battle of Messines 1918, the Battle of Hazebrouck, the Battle of Bailleul, the Action of Outtersteene Ridge, the capture of Ploegsteert and Hill 63, the Battle of Ypres 1918, the Battle of Courtrai.

11.11.1918 – Ended the war in Belgium, near Lessines.

1/4th 1/5th and 1/7th Battalions

04.08.1914 – The 1/4th was stationed at Winchester, the 1/5th at Carlton Place, Southampton and the 1/7th at Bournemouth; all part of the Hampshire Brigade of the Wessex Division and then moved on to Bulford.

09.10.1914 – Embarked for India from Southampton, where the Division was broken up.

Mar 1915 – Moved to Mesopotamia, landing at Basra and joining the 33rd Indian Brigade.

April 1915 – Transferred to the 30th Indian Brigade of the 12th Indian Division.

07.02.1915 – Defending HQ, except one company besieged in Kut al Amara until captured after their surrender.

May 1916 – Reconstituted and transferred to the 35th Brigade of the 14th Indian Division.

July 1916 – Transferred to the Corps Troops of the Tigris Corps.

Nov 1916 – Transferred to the 36th Indian Brigade of the 14th Indian Division.

31.10.1918 – Ended the war in Persia, Zenjan, south west of Resht near the Caspian Sea.

2/7th Battalion Territorial Force

Sep 1914 – In Bournemouth.

Oct 1914 – Joined the 2/1st Hampshire Brigade of the 2/Wessex Division.

13.12.1914 – Embarked for India from Southampton.

04.01.1915 – Arrived at Bombay where the Division was broken up, and drafts used to supply the Front Line.

Sep 1917 – Embarked for Mesopotamia, arriving at Basra.

Sep 1918 – Moved to defend the lines of communication and attached to the 38th Brigade of the 13th Division.

31.10.1918 – Ended the war in Mesopotamia, near Delli Abbas, north-east of Baghdad.

King's Own Yorkshire Light Infantry in World War I

9th & 10th (Service) Battalion

Sep 1914 – Both formed at Pontefract as part of the Third New Army (K3) and then moved to Berkhamsted to join the 64th Brigade of the 21st Division. They then moved to Halton Park, Tring.

Nov 1914 – Moved to Maidenhead.

Apr 1915 – Returned to Halton Park and then on to Witley.

Sep 1915 – Mobilised for war, landed in France and engaged in various actions on the Western Front including:

1915 – The Battle of Loos (the Division suffered severe casualties and took the rest of the year to rebuild).

1916 – The Battle of Albert, the Battle of Bazentin Ridge, the Battle of Flers-Courcelette, the Battle of Morval, the Battle of Le Transloy.

1917 – The German retreat to the Hindenburg Line, the First Battle of the Scarpe, the Third Battle of the Scarpe, the flanking operations around Bullecourt, the Battle of Polygon Wood, the Battle of Broodseinde, the Second Battle of Passchendaele, and the Cambrai Operations.

13.02.1918 – the 10th disbanded in France. The 9th continued to be engaged in action:

1918 – The Battle of St Quentin, the First Battle of Bapaume, the Battle of Messines, the Second Battle of Kemmel, the Battle of the Aisne 1918, the Battle of Albert, the Second Battle of Bapaume, the Battle of Epehy, the Battle of the St Quentin Canal, the Battle of Cambrai 1918, and the Battle of the Selle.

11.11.1918 – Ended the war moving to Limont-Fontaine, north east of Aulnoye, France.

King's Royal Rifle Corps during World War I

The regiment raised 22 Battalions in total during the course of World War I and saw action on the Western Front, Macedonia and Italy, achieving 60 battle honours including 7 Victoria Crosses. The regiment lost 12,840 men who were killed during the course of the war.

2nd Battalion

04.08.1914 – Stationed at Blackdown, Aldershot at the outbreak of war as part of the 2nd Brigade of the 1st Division.

13.08.1914 – Mobilised for war and landed at Le Havre. Engaged in various action on the Western Front including:

1914 – The Battle of Mons and the subsequent retreat, the Battle of the Marne, the Battle of the Aisne, the First Battle of Ypres.

1915 – Winter Operations 1914–15, the Battle of Aubers, the Battle of Loos.

1916 – The Battle of Albert, the Battle of Bazentin, the Battle of Pozières, the Battle of Flers-Courcelette, the Battle of Morval.

1917 – The German retreat to the Hindenburg Line, the Second Battle of Passchendaele.

1918 – The Battle of Estaires, the Battle of Hazebrouck, the Battle of Bethune, the Battle of Drocourt-Quéant, the Battle of Epehy, the Battle of the St Quentin Canal, the Battle of Beaurevoir, the Battle of the Selle, the Battle of the Sambre.

11.11.1918 – Ended the war in Fresnoy-le-Grand, France.

London Regiment during World War I

1/12th (City of London) Battalion (Kensington)

04.08.1914 – Stationed at Bedford Square as part of the 3rd London Brigade of the 1st London Division and then moved to Bullswater, Pirbright, Surrey and then Crowborough, Sussex.

Oct 1914 – Moved to a war station guarding the railway from Waterloo to North Camp, Hants and then moved to Roehampton.

Dec 1914 – Mobilised for war and embarked for France, leaving the 1st London Division and arriving at Le Havre. Moved to defend the lines of communication.

08.02.1915 – Transferred to the 84th Brigade of the 28th Division and engaged in actions on the Western Front including the Second Battle of Ypres.

20.05.1915 – Transferred to the GHQ Troops forming a composite battalion with the 1/5th and 1/3rd Battalions.

11.08.1915 – Resumed the battalion's identity for the Battle of Loos.

12.02.1916 – Transferred to the 168th Brigade of the 56th Division.

1916 – In January 1916 the War Office authorised the re-formation of the London Division, now to be known as the 56th, in France. They were involved in the diversionary attack at Gommecourt, the Battle of Ginchy, the Battle of Flers-Courcelette, the Battle of Morval, and the Battle of the Transloy Ridges.

1917 – The German retreat to the Hindenburg Line, the First Battle of the Scarpe, the Third Battle of the Scarpe, the Battle of Langemarck, the capture of Tadpole Copse, the capture of Bourlon Wood, and the German counter attacks.

31.01.1918 – Transferred to the 175th Brigade of the 58th Division, absorbing the 2/12th Battalion and becoming the 12th Battalion.

1918 – The Battle of St Quentin, the Battle of the Avre, the Battle of Villers-Bretonneux, the Battle of Amiens, the Battle of Albert, the Second Battle of Bapaume, the Battle of Epehy, and the general final advance in Artois.

11.11.1918 – Ended the war at Peruwelz area, south-east of Tournai, Belgium.

The Machine Gun Corps during World War I

The 98th Machine Gun Company, Machine Gun Corps joined 98th Brigade 33rd Division on 28th April 1916.

1916 – They were in action in the Battles of the Somme.

1917 – The Corps took part in the Arras Offensive, the actions on the Hindenburg Line, the operations on the Flanders coast and the Third Battles of Ypres.

19.02.18 – The men joined with the other machine gun companies of 33rd Division and became 33rd Battalion MGC.

Royal Engineers during World War I

Preparation for the Battle of Arras

Oct 1916 – From October 1916, the Royal Engineers had been working underground, constructing tunnels for the troops in preparation for the Battle of Arras in 1917. Beneath Arras itself, there is a vast network of caverns called The Boves, consisting of underground quarries and sewage tunnels. The engineers came up with a plan to add new tunnels to this network so that troops could arrive at the battlefield in secrecy and in safety. The size of the excavation was immense. In one sector alone four Tunnel Companies of 500 men each worked around the clock in 18-hour shifts for two months.

1917 – The Battle of Arras.

Royal Field Artillery during World War I

At the end of the 19th century The Royal Artillery was divided into Garrison and Field Artillery. The Royal Field Artillery was then divided into: Horse batteries, Field batteries and Mountain batteries.

The Royal Horse Artillery is dealt with under a separate section. The field batteries were numbered 1–103 and had their depot at Woolwich. A battery was commanded by a major with a captain as 2nd in command. It was divided into two or three sections, each commanded by a lieutenant and consisting of a detachment of two guns.

The field batteries were stationed around Britain, two or three being garrisoned together under a lieutenant-colonel. In a war situation, three batteries would form a brigade division and would be added to an infantry division.

There were ten Mountain batteries (numbered 1–10) and they served in India. Their uniform was the same as that of the Field Artillery, except for their lace boots and gaiters which were brown instead of black

The Royal Field Artillery provided support for the British Army. It came into being when the Royal Artillery was divided on 1st July 1899, and it was re-amalgamated back into the Royal Artillery in 1924.

The Royal Field Artillery was the largest arm of the artillery, responsible for the medium calibre guns and howitzers. They were deployed close to the front line and proved reasonably mobile. The Royal Field was organised into brigades, and attached to divisions or higher formations.

During the First World War a whole new form of artillery was developed to meet the unusual conditions of war on the Western Front; the trench mortar. With the lighter weapons being manned by the infantry, the Royal Field Artillery provided the manpower for the heavier mortars.

Royal Army Service Corps during World War I

The role of the RASC in the field fell into two main parts: supply and transport.

Supply: Supply embraced the provision of food, petrol and lubricants, fuel and light, hospital supplies and disinfectants.

Transport: Transport was concerned with the conveyance of the above supplies, together with ammunition, engineer and ordnance stores, and post, whether from the railhead, or from base if no railhead existed, to all units of a field force.

In addition, RASC units were provided for the carriage of infantry, tanks and heavy bridging equipment. The mechanical transport of medical and certain other units was also operated by the RASC.

To enable these services to be undertaken effectively, the RASC was responsible for the provision, repair, and maintenance of their own mechanical transport.

Personnel of the RASC were trained to fight as infantry and RASC units were responsible for their own local defence.

Divisional RASC

The role of the RASC companies was to keep the front-line units supplied. In order to do this there were three different operations carried out simultaneously. By the end of the campaign it was usual to have a company assigned to supplies, another to petrol and a third to ammunition.

Early in the campaign it was more usual to have companies serving brigades and have those companies each assign a platoon to supplies, petrol and ammunition. Clearly the brigade company allowed the brigade to operate independently and was well suited to the rapid advances of armoured divisions. In the large, and often fairly static, armies of the winter of 1944–45, the commodity company was more efficient. The supply system was overhauled in the autumn of 1944 when it became common for transport from army level to deliver to division refilling points, and thus cut out a stage of loading and unloading.

Rifle Brigade during World War I

The regiment formed a total of 28 battalions during the First World War, in addition to the pre-war establishment of two Regular, two Militia and two Territorial battalions. The regiment lost 11,575 men in the war and was awarded 52 battle honours, including 10 Victoria Crosses.

3rd Battalion

04.08.1914 – Stationed at Cork as part of the 17th Brigade of the 6th Division, then moved to Cambridge and afterwards went on to Newmarket.

12.09.1914 – Mobilised for war and landed at St Nazaire and took part in various actions on the Western Front including:

During 1914 – The action on the Aisne Heights, the Attack on Pérenchies.

Dec 1914 – This battalion took part in the Christmas Truce of 1914.

14.10.1915 – Transferred to the 17th Brigade of the 24th Division.

1915 – The Battle of Loos.

1916 – Action of the Bluff, the Battle of Devlin Wood.

1917 – The Battle of Arras, the Battle of Messines, the Battle of Pilckem Ridge, attack on Passchendaele.

1918 – Battle of the Somme at Falvy Bridge and Vrély, attack on St Aubert.

11.11.1918 – Ended the war in France, at Bavay.

Wiltshire Regiment during World War I

The Regiment raised 10 battalions, and gained 60 battle honours and 1 Victoria Cross. They were to lose 5,200 men during the course of the war.

5th (Service) Battalion

Aug 1914 – Formed at Devizes as part of the First New Army (K1) and then moved to Assaye Barracks, Tidworth as part of the 13th Division.

Oct 1914 – Moved to Chiseldon, Swindon.

Dec 1914 – Moved to Cirencester and joined the 40th Brigade of the 13th Division to replace the 7th Welsh Regiment.

Feb 1915 – Moved to Woking and then Bisley, both in Surrey.

01.07.1915 – Embarked for Gallipoli from Avonmouth via the Mediterranean and Mudros.

30.07.1915 – Landed at Helles.

04.08.1915 – Landed at Anzac and engaged in various actions against the Turkish Army including: The Battle of Sari Bair, the Battle of Russell's Top, the Battle of Hill 60.

Jan 1916 – Evacuated from Gallipoli to Egypt due to severe casualties from combat, disease and harsh weather.

Feb 1916 – Deployed to Mesopotamia and involved in various actions against the Turkish Army.

1917 – The Battle of Kut al Amara, the capture of the Hai Salient, the capture of Dahra Bend, the passage of the Diyala, the pursuit of the enemy towards Baghdad, Capture of Baghdad, Battles of Delli 'Abbas, Duqma, Nahr Kalis, crossed the 'Adhaim and at Shatt al 'Adhaim, the Second and Third Actions of Jabal Hamrin and at Tuz Khurmatli.

1918 – In operations as part of 'Lewin's Column', pushing north towards Turkey.

31.10.1918 – Ended the war at Altun Kupri north of Kirkuk, Mesopotamia

Worcestershire Regiment during WWI

14th (Service) Battalion (Severn Valley Pioneers)

10.09.1915 – Formed at Worcester by Lt Col H Webb MP.

Mar 1916 – Taken over by the War Office and moved to Salisbury Plain.

21.06.1916 – Mobilised for war and landed at Le Havre, where they joined the 63rd Division, to engage in action on the Western Front that included:

Nov 1916 – The Battle of the Ancre.

1917 – The operations on the Ancre, the Second Battle of the Scarpe, the Arras Offensive when the division captured Gavrelle, the Battle of Arleux, the Second Battle of Passchendaele, the Third Battle of Ypres, the Action of Welsh Ridge and the Cambrai operations.

1918 – The Battle of St Quentin, the Battle of Bapaume, the Battle of Albert, the Second Battle of the Somme 1918, the Battle of Drocourt-Quéant, the Second Battle of Arras, the Battle of the Canal du Nord, the Battle of Cambrai, the Passage of the Grand Honelle, and the Final Advance in Picardy.

11.11.1918 – Ended the war in Belgium, at Bougnies, south of Mons.

Yorkshire Regiment during World War I

The regiment is perhaps better known as the 'Green Howards'. This title dates back to the wars of Austrian Succession in the mid-1700s. The Colonel at the time was named Howard. At that time, regiments were often referred to by the name of their Colonel. As the regiment was brigaded with another, whose name was also Howard, there was duplication. So this regiment, which wore green facings to its uniform, became the 'Green' Howards and the other regiment the 'Buff' Howards. The Green Howards and the Buffs were names still in use in 1914–18.

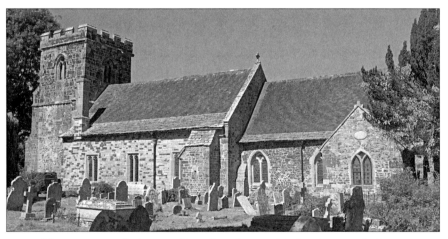

Hampreston All Saints Church – this used to be the parish church

WORLD WAR II

The Dorset Regiment in World War II

1st Battalion

1939 –The 1st Battalion of the Dorsets were sent to Malta to garrison the strategically important island in the middle of Rommel's Africa Corps supply route. Along with the 2nd Devons they endured the bombing by the Luftwaffe on the besieged island and shared the suffering of the Maltese people, until the Allies gained superiority in the Mediterranean in 1943.

Jul 1943 – When the Allies invaded Sicily in July, The Dorsets alongside The Devons took part in their first amphibious assault landing.

Sep 1943 – A second landing followed on the mainland of Italy at Porto Venere on 8th September. The stay in Italy was to be short-lived; the two battalions were brought home – their experience of assault landings was to spearhead the D-Day invasion of France as part of the 50th Division. Having landed slightly to the east of their objective at Le Hamel, on a beach that was still under enemy fire, they made their way inland and, by nightfall, were in and around the village of Ryes. The Dorsets then advanced towards Bayeux.

The 1st Dorsets also took part in the battles fought around Tilly, Hottot and the Falaise Pocket. The 43rd Wessex Division carried out an assault river crossing of the Seine and quickly advanced across northern France. The 1st Dorsets and 2nd Devons fought their last battle together at Aam, Holland.

Hampshire Regiment in World War II

2nd Battalion

Aug 1939 – The battalion was in Aldershot, Hampshire.

13.09.39 – The battalion was sent to France as part of the BEF attached to the 1st Guards Brigade, 1st Division.

10.10.39 – They had moved to the Belgian/French border.

04.02.40 – The battalion stayed for three weeks on the Maginot Line.

11.05.40 – Due to the invasion of Belgium by the Germans, the battalion went into Belgium in response.

16.05.40 – The men were ordered to retreat.

01–02.06.40 – Evacuated from Dunkirk and returned to England, where the battalion was reinforced and re-equipped.

11.01.42 – Set sail for Africa to take part in 'Operation Torch'.

21.11.42 – Landed at Algiers.

29.11.42 – Battalion then moved to Tebourba. The next day they were heavily attacked by shelling.

01.12.42 – Came under heavy attack by a force four times its size. After three days the battalion was forced back and retreated through Tebourba. By now all the other troops had been withdrawn and the road behind them had been cut off. Some of the battalion managed to break through enemy lines but many were captured.

13.05.43 – After the fall of Tunis, the battalion had become attached to 128 (Hampshire) Brigade, 46th Division and took part in the Salerno landing. They went on to fight in the Italian campaign, attached to the same brigade, including in battles at Monte Ornito and at Monte Cassino.

Queen's Own (Royal West Kent Regiment) during WWII

4th Battalion

1940 – The battalion was part of the 132nd (Kent) Brigade. It was sent to France attached to the 44th (Home Counties) Division and was part of the British Expeditionary Force.

May–Jun 1940 – Along with the same division, they were evacuated from Dunkirk and returned to the UK where the battalion remained for a couple years.

May 1942 – Shipped out to North Africa.

Jul 1942 – Had arrived with the 5th Battalion in Egypt. They joined the 8th Army and fought at the Battles of Alam Halfa and Alamein.

Royal Artillary

Before the Second World War, Royal Artillery recruits were required to be at least 5ft 4ins tall and men in mechanised units had to be at least 5ft 8ins tall. In 1938, the Royal Artillery Brigades were renamed Regiments. In the Second World War more than a million men were serving in over 960 Gunner regiments. With the coming of  peace, the Gunners reduced to 250,000 men and 365 batteries in 106 regiments.

At the beginning of 1939, the regular and TA strength of the Royal Artillery totalled about 105,000. In mid-1943 the RA reached its peak strength, some 700,000 strong (about 26% of the total British Army and about the same size as the Royal Navy), including about 5% of officers in some 630 regiments, 65 training regiments and six officer cadet training units.

These included 130 regiments converted from TA infantry and yeomanry, often retaining their previous regimental title as part of their artillery unit designation as well as badges and other accoutrements. However, the strength of the field branch (including anti-tank) in mid-1943 was about 232,000. The regiment suffered some 31,000 fatalities during the course of the war.

Of the 630 or so regiments about 240 were field artillery, excluding about 60 anti-tank ones. At the end of the Second World War, the RA was larger in numbers than the Royal Navy.

Royal Army Medical Corps

The Royal Army Medical Corps (RAMC) is a specialist corps in the army, which provides medical services to all British armed personnel and their families in war and in peacetime. Together with the Royal Army Veterinary Corps, the Royal Army Dental Corps and Queen Alexandra's Royal Army Nursing Corps, the RAMC forms the British Army's essential medical services.

The RAMC does not carry a Regimental or Queen's Colour, although it has a Regimental flag. Nor does it have battle honours, as elements of the corps have been present in almost every single war the army has fought. Because it is not a fighting arm, under the Geneva Conventions, members of the RAMC may only use their weapons for self-defence. For this reason, there are two traditions that the RAMC perform when on parade:

- officers do not draw their swords – instead they hold their scabbard with their left hand while saluting with their right

- other ranks do not fix bayonets.

Unlike medical officers in some other countries, medical officers in the RAMC (and the Royal Navy and Royal Air Force) do not use the 'Dr' prefix, in parentheses or otherwise but only their rank, although they may be addressed informally as 'Doctor'.

Royal Army Service Corps

The role of the RASC in the field falls into two main parts – supply and transport. **Supply:** Supply embraces the provision of food, petrol and lubricants, fuel and light, hospital supplies and disinfectants.

Transport: Transport is concerned with the conveyance of the above supplies, together with ammunition, engineer stores, ordnance stores and post, from the railhead, or from base if no railhead exists, to all units of a field force.

In addition, RASC units are provided for the carriage of infantry, tanks and heavy bridging equipment. The mechanical transport of medical and certain other units is also found and operated by the RASC.

To enable these services to be undertaken effectively, the RASC are responsible for the provision, repair, and maintenance of their own mechanical transport.

General Transport Companies are allotted to divisions for the transport of ammunition, supplies and petrol. Similar companies are allotted to higher formations and for employment in line of communication areas as required.

Personnel of the RASC are trained to fight as infantry and RASC units are responsible for their own local defence.

Royal Tank Regiment

The Royal Tank Regiment is an armoured regiment, previously known as the Tank Corps and the Royal Tank Corps. The RTR is part the Royal Armoured Corps and is made up of two operational regiments; the 1st Royal Tank Regiment and the 2nd Royal Tank Regiment.

The corps has had more regiments over time with up to the 8th RTR.

In 1923, it was officially named Royal (making it the Royal Tank Corps) by Colonel-in-Chief King George V. It was at this time that the motto 'Fear Naught', the black beret and the unit badge were adopted. The word Corps was replaced in 1939 with Regiment to give the unit its current name, the Royal Tank Regiment.

In 1920, 12 Armoured Car Companies were set up as part of the Tank Corps, absorbing units from the Machine Gun Corps; eight were later converted into independent Light Tank Companies. All disbanded before the outbreak of the Second World War.

In 1933, the 6th Battalion, Royal Tank Corps, was formed in Egypt by combining the personnel of two of these companies; in 1934, the 1st (Light) Battalion, Royal Tank Corps was formed in England with personnel from three of the existing battalions.

With the preparations for war in the late 1930s, a further two regular battalions were formed; the 7th in 1937 and the 8th in 1938. The 40th, 41st, 42nd, 43rd, 44th and 45th battalions were raised in 1938, being converted from Territorial Army infantry battalions; the 46th, 47th, 48th, 49th, 50th and 51st were likewise activated and converted in 1939. The twelve Yeomanry Armoured Car Companies of the RTR were all activated and transferred to the Royal Armoured Corps.

Before the Second World War, Royal Tank Corps recruits were required to be at least 5ft 4in tall. They initially enlisted for six years with the colours and a further six years with the reserve.

Royal Air Force

While the British were not the first to make use of heavier-than-air military aircraft, the RAF is the world's oldest independent air force; that is, the first air force to become independent of army or navy control. It was founded on 1st April 1918, with headquarters located in the former Hotel Cecil, during the First World War, by the amalgamation of the Royal Flying Corps (RFC)  and the Royal Naval Air Service (RNAS). After the first war, the service was drastically cut and its inter-war years were relatively quiet, with the RAF taking responsibility for the control of Iraq and executing a number of minor actions in other parts of the British Empire. Naval aviation in the form of the RAF's Fleet Air Arm was returned to Admiralty control on 24th May 1939.

The RAF developed its doctrine of strategic bombing which led to the construction of long-range bombers and became the basic philosophy in the Second World War.

The RAF underwent rapid expansion prior to, and during, the Second World War. Under the British Commonwealth Air Training Plan of December 1939, the air forces of British Commonwealth countries trained and formed 'Article XV squadrons' for service with RAF formations. Many individual personnel from these countries, and exiles from occupied Europe, also served with RAF squadrons.

In the Battle of Britain, in the late summer of 1940, the RAF (supplemented by two Fleet Air Arm Squadrons, Polish, Czechoslovakian and other multinational pilots and ground personnel) defended the skies over Britain against the German Luftwaffe, helping foil Hitler's plans for an invasion of Britain and prompting Prime Minister Winston Churchill to say in the House of Commons on 20th August: 'Never in the field of human conflict was so much owed by so many to so few'.

The largest RAF effort during the war was the strategic bombing campaign against Germany by Bomber Command. While RAF bombing of Germany began almost immediately upon the outbreak of war, under the leadership of Air Chief Marshal Harris, these attacks became increasingly devastating from 1942 onwards as new technology and greater numbers of superior aircraft became available. The RAF adopted night-time area bombing on German cities such as Hamburg and Dresden, and developed precision bombing techniques for specific operations, such as the 'Dambusters' raid by No 617 Squadron, or the Amiens prison raid known as Operation Jericho.

Royal Air Force Volunteer Reserve

The RAFVR was formed in July 1936 to provide individuals to supplement the Auxiliary Air Force (AAF) which had been formed in 1925 by the local Territorial Associations. The AAF was organised on a squadron basis, with local recruitment similar to the Territorial Army regiments. Initially the RAFVR was composed of civilians recruited from the neighbourhoods of Reserve Flying Schools, which were run by civilian contractors largely employed as instructor members of the Reserve of Air Force Officers (RAFO), who had previously completed a four-year short service commission as pilots in the RAF. Navigation instructors were mainly former master mariners without any air experience. Recruits were confined to men of between 18 and 25 years of age who had been accepted for part-time training as pilots, observers and wireless operators. The object was to provide a reserve of aircrew for use in the event of war. By September 1939, the RAFVR comprised 6,646 pilots, 1,625 observers and 1,946 wireless operators.

When war broke out in 1939, the Air Ministry employed the RAFVR as the principal means for aircrew entry to serve with the RAF. A civilian volunteer on being accepted for aircrew training took an oath of allegiance (attestation) and was then inducted into the RAFVR. Normally the volunteer returned to their civilian job for several months until called up for aircrew training. During this waiting period, the aircrew member could wear a silver RAFVR lapel badge to indicate their status.

By the end of 1941 more than half of Bomber Command aircrew were members of the RAFVR. Most of the pre-war pilot and observer NCO aircrew had been commissioned and the surviving regular officers and members of the RAFO filled the posts of flight and squadron commanders. Eventually, of the aircrew in the Command, probably more than 95% were serving members of the RAFVR.

During 1943, the decision was taken by the Air Ministry to raise an order for members of the RAFVR to remove the brass and cloth 'VR's worn on the collars and shoulders of officers and other ranks (respectively), as these were viewed as being divisive. No similar order was raised for members of the Auxiliary Air Force, who retained their 'A's on uniforms at that time.

Royal Navy

The Royal Navy is the naval warfare service branch of the British Armed Forces. Founded in the 16th century, it is the oldest service branch and is therefore known as the Senior Service. From the end of the 17th century until well into the 20th century, it was seen as the most powerful navy in the world, playing a key part in establishing the British Empire as the dominant world power.

After World War II the Royal Navy was replaced by the United States Navy as the world's foremost naval power. During the Cold War it was transformed into a primarily anti-submarine force, hunting for Soviet submarines, mostly active in the Greenland, Iceland, UK (GIUK) gap. This relates to the stretch of water between these countries. With the collapse of the Soviet Union, the Royal Navy's role for the 21st century has returned to focusing on global expeditionary operations.

APPENDIX 2

WAR MEMORIALS AND CEMETERIES LISTED IN THIS BOOK

WORLD WAR I

AMARA WAR CEMETERY

Country: Iraq
Identified casualties: 3,696

Location information

Amara is a town on the left bank of the Tigris some 520km from the sea. The War Cemetery is a little east of the town between the left bank of the river and the Chahaila Canal.

Visiting information

While the current climate of political instability persists it is not possible for the Commonwealth War Graves Commission to manage or maintain its cemeteries and memorials located within Iraq. Alternative arrangements for commemoration have therefore been implemented and a two volume Roll of Honour, listing all casualties buried and commemorated in Iraq has been produced. These volumes are on display at the Commission's Head Office in Maidenhead and are available for the public to view.

Historical information

Amara was occupied by the Mesopotamian Expeditionary Force on 3rd June 1915 and it immediately became a hospital centre. The accommodation for medical units on both banks of the Tigris was greatly increased during 1916 and, in April 1917, seven general hospitals and some smaller units were stationed there.

Amara War Cemetery contains 4,621 burials from the First World War, more than 3,000 of which were brought into the cemetery after the Armistice. Some 925 of the graves are unidentified. In 1933, all of the headstones were removed from this cemetery when it was discovered that salts in the soil were causing them to deteriorate. Instead a screen wall was erected with the names of those buried engraved upon it. Plot XXV is a Collective Grave, the individual burial places within this are not known.

There are also seven non-war graves in the cemetery.

AUCHONVILLERS MILITARY CEMETERY

Country: France
Locality: Somme
Identified casualties: 486

Location information

Auchonvillers is approximately 20km south of Arras. Taking the D919 from Arras to Amiens you will drive through the villages of Bucquoy, Puisieux then Serre-les-Puisieux. On leaving the last, going 3km further along the D919, turn left following the signs for Auchonvillers. At the crossroads in the village centre follow the CWGC signs for Auchonvillers Military Cemetery which is on the outskirts of the village on the right-hand side.

Historical information

From the outbreak of the war to the summer of 1915, this part of the front was held by French troops, who started the military cemetery in June 1915. It continued to be used by Commonwealth field ambulances and fighting units, but burials practically ceased with the German withdrawal in February 1917. After the Armistice, 15 of the graves (Plot II, Row M, Graves 4–18) were brought in from scattered positions east of the cemetery.

The cemetery now contains 528 Commonwealth burials of the First World War, the French graves having been removed to other burial grounds.

The cemetery was designed by Sir Reginald Blomfield.

BAGNEUX BRITISH CEMETERY, GEZAINCOURT

Country: France
Locality: Somme
Identified casualties: 1,371

Location information

Gezaincourt is a village situated 2km to the south west of the town of Doullens. Bagneux British Cemetery lies to the south of the village. There is a Commonwealth War Graves Commission signpost in Gezaincourt village opposite the 'Chateau' entrance.

Historical information

The cemetery was begun in April 1918 after the close of the German offensive in Picardy. At the end of March, the 3rd, 29th and 56th Casualty Clearing Stations had come to Gezaincourt, where they were joined for a short time in April by the 45th. They remained until September. The 3rd Canadian Stationary Hospital, in the citadel at Doullens, also buried casualties in this cemetery in May and June 1918, and the 2nd Canadian Division in April and May. The graves in Plot III, Row A, relate to a bombing raid over Doullens on 30th May 1918.

There are 1,374 servicemen of the First World War buried or commemorated in the cemetery.

The cemetery was designed by Sir Edwin Lutyens.

BASRA MEMORIAL

Country: Iraq
Identified casualties: 40,626

Location information

Until 1997, the Basra Memorial was located on the main quay of the naval dockyard at Maqil, on the west bank of the Shatt-al-Arab, about 8km north of Basra.

Because of the sensitivity of the site, the memorial was moved by presidential decree. The move, carried out by the authorities in Iraq, involved a considerable amount of manpower, transport costs and sheer engineering on their part, and the memorial has been re-erected in its entirety.

The Basra Memorial is now located 32km along the road to Nasiriyah, in the middle of what was a major battleground during the first Gulf War.

The panel numbers quoted at the end of each entry relate to the panels dedicated to the regiment served with.

Visiting information

While the current climate of political instability persists it is not possible for the Commission to manage or maintain its cemeteries and memorials located within Iraq. Alternative arrangements for commemoration have therefore been implemented and a two-volume Roll of Honour listing all casualties buried and commemorated in Iraq has been produced. These volumes are on display at the Commission's Head Office in Maidenhead and are available for the public to view.

Historical information

The Basra Memorial commemorates more than 40,500 members of the Commonwealth forces who died in the operations in Mesopotamia from the autumn of 1914 to the end of August 1921 and whose graves are not known.

The memorial was designed by Edward Warren and unveiled by Sir Gilbert Clayton on 27th March 1929.

BRAY BRITISH CEMETERY, BRAY-SUR-SOMME

Country: France
Locality: Somme
Identified casualties: 107

Location information

Bray-sur-Somme is a village and commune in the Department of the Somme, 8km south east of Albert and 16km west of Péronne. Bray Vale British Cemetery is on the east side of the town of Albert.

Historical information

Bray-sur-Somme fell into German hands in March 1918, but it was retaken by the 40th Australian Battalion on the following 24th August.

Bray Vale British Cemetery (previously named Bray No 2 British Cemetery) consisted originally of the 25 graves (from August 1918) in Plot II, Row A, but it was enlarged soon after the Armistice when further graves were brought in from the neighbourhood. In 1923 the space between the cemetery and the road, now Plots III and IV, was filled by graves brought in mainly from the battlefields of 1916 round Thiepval and Courcelette.

The cemetery contains 279 First World War burials, 172 of them unidentified.

The cemetery was designed by AJS Hutton.

CERISY-GAILLY MILITARY CEMETERY

Country: France
Locality: Somme
Identified casualties: 631

Location information

Cerisy is a village 10km south west of Albert.

From Albert take the D42 in the direction of Morlancourt and Moreuil. After passing Morlancourt you arrive at Sailly-Laurette. Continue until reaching

a crossroads where you turn left onto the D71 in the direction of Cerisy. Continue on the D71 until you approach a group of bungalows on your left. Turn left at the end of the bungalows. You will then approach Cerisy-Gailly Military Cemetery.

Historical information

Gailly was the site of the 39th and 13th Casualty Clearing Stations during the early part of 1917, and of the 41st Stationary Hospital from May 1917 to March 1918. The villages were then captured by the Germans, but were retaken by the Australian Corps in August 1918.

Cerisy-Gailly Military Cemetery (originally called the New French Military Cemetery) was created in February 1917 and used by medical units until March 1918. After the recapture of the village it was used by Australian units. The cemetery was increased after the Armistice when graves were brought in from the battlefields of the Somme and some smaller cemeteries.

DOZINGHEM MILITARY CEMETERY

Country:	Belgium
Locality:	Poperinghe, West-Vlaanderen
Identified casualties:	3,240

Location information

The cemetery is to the north west of Poperinghe near Krombeke. From Ieper, follow the directions to Poperinghe along the by-pass. At the end of the by-pass turn right at the traffic lights into Oostlaan. Follow Oostlaan over the roundabout to the end of  the road. Turn left into Veurnestraat and go along to the first turning on the right. (From Poperinghe centre, follow the directions to Veurne along the Veurnestraat to the second turning on the left.) Turn into Sint-Bertinusstraat and follow this road up the rise and around a left-hand bend. After the bend, take the right-hand turning in the direction of Krombeke along the Krombeekseweg. Follow the Krombeekseweg past the 'De Lovie' centre where the road name changes to Leeuwerikstraat and then past a café on the left. Approximately 500m after the café, you will see a sign for the cemetery pointing to a track on the right leading into the woods. The cemetery is at the end of the track.

Historical information

Westvleteren was outside the Front held by Commonwealth forces in Belgium during the First World War but in July 1917, in readiness for the forthcoming offensive, groups of casualty clearing stations were placed at three positions called by the troops 'Mendinghem', 'Dozinghem' and 'Bandaghem'.

The 4th, 47th and 61st Casualty Clearing Stations were posted at Dozinghem and the military cemetery was used by them until early in 1918.

There are now 3,174 Commonwealth burials of the First World War in the cemetery and 65 German war graves from this period. The cemetery also contains 73 Second World War burials dating from the Allied withdrawal to Dunkirk in May 1940.

The cemetery was designed by Sir Reginald Blomfield.

ENGLEBELMER COMMUNAL CEMETERY

Country: France

Locality: Somme

Identified casualties: 51

Location information

Englebelmer is a village in the Department of the Somme, 8km north west of Albert and 24km south east of Arras. The cemetery is by the side of the road, with the British plots at the east end – to the right and left of the entrance.

The extension is at the south-west corner of the Communal Cemetery away from the road.

Historical information

The village of Englebelmer was in Allied hands during the whole of the War and was used as a Field Ambulance station; however, until the autumn of 1916, and again in the summer of 1918, it was liable to occasional shelling. It was later 'adopted' by the City of Winchester.

The Communal Cemetery was used for British burials from June to September 1916, and again in April and May 1918.

There are now over 50, 1914–18 war casualties commemorated at this site.

FAUBOURG D'AMIENS CEMETERY, ARRAS

Country: France

Locality: Pas de Calais

Identified casualties: 2,647

Location information

Faubourg-d'Amiens Cemetery is in the western part of the town of Arras in the Boulevard du General de Gaulle. It is near the Citadel, and roughly 2km west of the railway station.

Historical information

The French handed over Arras to Commonwealth forces in the spring of 1916, and the system of tunnels upon which the town is built were used and developed in preparation for the major offensive planned for April 1917.

The Commonwealth section of the Faubourg d'Amiens Cemetery was begun in March 1916, behind the existing French military cemetery. It continued to be used by field ambulances and fighting units until November 1918. The cemetery was enlarged after the Armistice, when graves were relocated from the battlefields and from two smaller cemeteries in the vicinity.

The cemetery contains over 2,650 Commonwealth burials of the First World War, 10 of which are unidentified. The graves in the French military cemetery were removed after the war to other burial grounds and the land they had occupied was used for the construction of the Arras Memorial and Arras Flying Services Memorial.

The adjacent Arras Memorial commemorates almost 35,000 servicemen from the UK, South Africa and New Zealand. These troops died in the Arras sector between the spring of 1916 and 7th August 1918, the eve of the Advance to Victory, and have no known grave. The most conspicuous events of this period were the Arras Offensive of April–May 1917, and the German attack in the spring of 1918. Canadian and Australian servicemen killed in these operations are commemorated by memorials at Vimy and Villers-Bretonneux. A separate memorial remembers those killed in the Battle of Cambrai in 1917.

GROVE TOWN CEMETERY, MEAULTE

Country: France

Locality: Somme

Identified casualties: 1,391

Location information

Méaulte is a village just south
of Albert. From Albert head
south east on the D329 in the
direction of Bray-sur-Somme.
Just before the main buildings for
the Aerobus, turn right for the
centre of Méaulte. Approximately
200m west of the church, take the
road south 'Rue de Etinehem'.

Continue south past Méaulte Military Cemetery, and approximately
2.3km further on, turn left (eastwards). Grove Town Cemetery is 600m
along on the right-hand side of this track.

For those wishing to approach the cemetery from the south side, take
the D1 Bray-sur-Somme/Corbie road, at the junction of the D1 and
C2 Etinehem/Méaulte minor road. Head north towards Méaulte, until
reaching a fork in the road, where there is a CWGC road sign. Take
the right fork in the direction of the airfield perimeter fence. At the
Commission road sign, take the left track north. Grove Town Cemetery
is ahead and to the left of the track.

Historical information

In September 1916, the 34th and 2/2nd London Casualty Clearing
Stations were established at this point, known to the troops as Grove
Town, to deal with casualties from the Somme battlefields. They were
moved in April 1917 and, except for a few burials in August and September
1918, the cemetery was closed.

Grove Town Cemetery contains 1,395 First World War burials. The
cemetery was designed by Sir Edwin Lutyens.

HELLES MEMORIAL

Country: Turkey (including Gallipoli)

Identified casualties: 20,878

Location information

The Anzac and Suvla cemeteries are first signposted from the left-hand junction of the Eceabat – Bigali Road. From this junction travel into the main Anzac area.

Follow the road to Helles, opposite the Kabatepe Museum at 14.2km. Take a right turn at the T-junction and at 14.3km, take the left fork. After a total of 22.8km, take a right turn to the memorial along a rough track 500m long.

The Helles Memorial stands on the tip of the Gallipoli Peninsula. It takes the form of an obelisk over 30m high that can be seen by ships passing through the Dardanelles.

Historical information

The eight-month campaign in Gallipoli was fought by Commonwealth and French forces in an attempt to force Turkey out of the war, to relieve the deadlock of the Western Front in France and Belgium, and to open a supply route to Russia through the Dardanelles and the Black Sea.

The Allies landed on the peninsula on 25th–26th April 1915; the 29th Division at Cape Helles in the south, and the Australian and New Zealand Corps north of Gaba Tepe (Kabatepe) on the west coast, an area soon known as Anzac. On 6th August further landings were made at Suvla, just north of Anzac, and the climax of the campaign came in early August when simultaneous assaults were launched on all three fronts. However, the difficult terrain and stiff Turkish resistance soon led to the stalemate of trench warfare. From the end of August, no further serious action was fought and the lines remained unchanged. The peninsula was successfully evacuated in December and early January 1916.

The Helles Memorial serves the dual function of Commonwealth battle memorial for the whole Gallipoli campaign and place of commemoration for many of those Commonwealth servicemen who died there and have no known grave.

The United Kingdom and Indian forces named on the memorial died in operations throughout the peninsula, the Australians at Helles. There are also panels for those who died or were buried at sea in Gallipoli waters. The memorial bears more than 21,000 names.

JANVAL CEMETERY, DIEPPE

Country:	France
Locality:	Seine-Maritime
Identified casualties:	234

Location information

Dieppe is a seaport at the mouth of the River Arques. Janval is one of the suburbs of Dieppe and the Janval Cemetery is one of the town's burial grounds. It is situated to the south west of the port area.

From the town square – the Place du Martyrs – head south on the Avenue Gambetta (direction Rouen), then take the 3rd exit on your right into the Avenue Boucher-de-Perthes. The cemetery entrance is at the end of this road on the Rue Montigny. There is a CWGC sign at the entrance.

Historical information

Dieppe was used by Commonwealth forces as a minor base from December 1914 onwards, particularly for supplies of small arms ammunition, forage and flour. From January 1915 to May 1919, 'A' Section of No 5 Stationary Hospital was based in the town.

During this period, 219 Commonwealth burials were made in Janval Cemetery, a large civil burial ground. Most of the graves form two plots in Section T, but there are also three burials among the French and Belgian military graves in Section U.

KIRKEE 1914–1918 MEMORIAL

Country: India
Identified casualties: 735

Location information

Kirkee, also known as Khadki, is a military camp adjoining the large university town of Poona on the Plateau above Bombay. It can be reached by train from Bombay to Poona or by long distance taxi service from Bombay. There are direct flights from Bombay, Madras and Delhi but these tend to be irregular.

Taxis and motor rickshaws are available from Poona Railway Station. To reach Kirkee War Cemetery, in which the memorial stands, ask for Mula Road where the cemetery is located. One way is to cross the Sangam Bridge and follow the road, which has the River Mula on its right. The CWGC road direction board is on a crossroads with the Bombay Poona Road. The cemetery is situated on the right-hand side and backs onto the river.

From the railway station follow the way via Juna Bazar, Sangam Bridge, past the Engineering College, over Wakdewadi Bridge, past Bajaj Kamal Nayan Udyan and onto Bhayawadi and Mula Roads.

From the airport, travel via Ahmadnagar Road, which joins onto Nagar Road, followed by Deccan College Road. Go over the Holkar Bridge and, keeping left at the junction with Elphinson Road, you enter Mula Road. The cemetery is a short distance away on the left-hand side of the road. The Commonwealth War Graves road direction sign is situated at the junctions of Elphinson Road and Mula Road but it should be noted that this is often hidden from view.

Historical information

The Kirkee 1914–1918 Memorial commemorates more than 1,800 servicemen and women who died in India during the First World War, who are buried in civil and cantonment cemeteries in India and Pakistan where their graves were considered to be unmaintainable. The Commission is currently working to reinstate the original graves of a large number of the individuals commemorated here, and as a result the official commemoration of some of these individuals has been reverted back to their original burial location, although their names will still remain on the Kirkee 1914–1918 Memorial for the foreseeable future. This total also includes the names of 629 servicemen whose remains were brought from Bombay (Sewri) Cemetery for re-interment here in 1962, and are buried in the grassed area between the Memorial and the Cross of Sacrifice.

LE TOURET MEMORIAL

Country: France

Locality: Pas de Calais

Identified casualties: 13,393

Location information

Le Touret Memorial is located at the east end of Le Touret Military Cemetery, on the south side of the Bethune-Armentières main road.

From Bethune follow the signs for Armentières until you are on the D171. Continue on this road through Essars and Le Touret village. Approximately 1km after Le Touret village and about 5km before you reach the intersection with the D947, Estaires to La Bassée road, the Cemetery lies on the right-hand side of the road.

The memorial takes the form of a loggia surrounding an open rectangular court. The court is enclosed by three solid walls and on the eastern side by a colonnade. East of the colonnade is a wall and the colonnade and wall are prolonged northwards (to the road) and southwards, forming a long gallery. Small pavilions mark the ends of the gallery and the western corners of the court.

Historical information

The Le Touret Memorial

The Le Touret Memorial commemorates over 13,400 British soldiers who were killed in this sector of the Western Front from the beginning of October 1914 to the eve of the Battle of Loos in late September 1915 and who have no known grave. The memorial takes the form of a loggia surrounding an open rectangular court. The names of those commemorated are listed on panels set into the walls of the court and the gallery, arranged by regiment, rank and alphabetically by surname within the rank. This memorial was designed by John Reginald Truelove, who had served as an officer with the London Regiment during the war, and it was unveiled by the British ambassador to France, Lord Tyrrell, on 22nd March 1930.

Almost all of the men commemorated on the memorial served with regular or territorial regiments from across the UK and were killed in actions that took place along a section of the front line that stretched from Estaires in the north to Grenay in the south. This part of the Western Front was the scene of some of the heaviest fighting of the first year of the war, including the battles of La Bassée (10th October – 2nd November 1914), Neuve Chapelle (10th–12th March 1915), Aubers Ridge (9th–10th May 1915), and Festubert (15th–25th May 1915). Soldiers serving with Indian and Canadian units who were killed in this sector in 1914–15, whose remains were never identified, are commemorated on the Neuve Chapelle and Vimy memorials, while those who fell during the northern pincer attack at the Battle of Aubers Ridge are commemorated on the Ploegsteert Memorial.

Le Touret Military Cemetery

The men of the Indian Corps began burying their fallen comrades at this site in November 1914, and the cemetery was used continually by field ambulances and fighting units until the German spring offensive began in March 1918. Richebourg L'Avoué was overrun by the German forces in April 1918, but the cemetery was used again in September and October after this territory was recaptured by the Allies. Today over 900 Commonwealth servicemen who were killed during the First World War are buried here.

LIJSSENTHOEK MILITARY CEMETERY

Country:	Belgium
Locality:	Poperinghe, West-Vlaanderen
Identified casualties:	9,877

Location information

Lijssenthoek Military Cemetery is located 12km west of Ieper town centre, on the Boescheepseweg, a road leading from the N308 connecting Ieper to Poperinghe.

From Ieper town centre the Poperingseweg (N308) is reached via the Elverdingestraat, then go over two small roundabouts in the J Capronstraat. The Poperingseweg is a continuation of the J Capronstraat and begins after a railway level crossing.

On reaching Poperinghe, the N308 joins the left-hand turning onto the R33, Poperinghe ring road. The R33 continues to the left-hand junction with the N38 Frans-Vlaanderenweg. 800m along the N38 lies the left turn onto Lenestraat. The next immediate right-hand turning leads onto Boescheepseweg. The cemetery itself is located 2km along Boescheepseweg on the right-hand side of the road.

Historical information

During the First World War, the village of Lijssenthoek was situated on the main communication line between the Allied military bases in the rear and the Ypres battlefields. Close to the Front, yet out of the extreme range of most German field artillery, it became a natural place to establish casualty clearing stations. The cemetery was first used by the French 15th Hôpital D'évacuation and, in June 1915, it began to be used by casualty clearing stations of the Commonwealth forces.

From April to August 1918, the casualty clearing stations fell back before the German advance and field ambulances (including a French ambulance) took their places.

The cemetery contains 9,901 Commonwealth burials of the First World War, with 24 being unidentified. There are 883 war graves of other nationalities, mostly French and German, 11 of these are unidentified. There is one non-World War burial here.

The only concentration burials were 24 added to Plot XXXI in 1920 from isolated positions near Poperinghe and 17 that were added to Plot XXXII from St Denijs Churchyard in 1981.

Eight of the headstones are special memorials to men known to be buried in this cemetery, these are located together alongside Plot 32 near the Stone of Remembrance.

The cemetery, designed by Sir Reginald Blomfield, is the second largest Commonwealth cemetery in Belgium.

DEVONSHIRE CEMETERY, MAMETZ

Country: France

Locality: Somme

Identified casualties: 153

Location information

Mametz is a village in the Department of the Somme, 6.5km east of Albert.

Devonshire Cemetery is 800m south of Mametz and is situated on high ground some 450m west of the road (D938) from Albert to Péronne, 6.5km from Albert.

Historical information

Mametz was within the German lines until 1st July 1916 when it was captured by the 7th Division, and Mametz Wood, north-east of the village, was cleared on the days following 7th July.

The 8th and 9th Battalions of the Devonshire Regiments, which were part of the 7th Division, attacked on 1st July 1916 from a point on the south-west side of Albert-Maricourt road, due south of Mametz village. It was by a plantation called Mansel Copse. On 4th July they returned to this location and established a cemetery, burying their dead in a section of their old front-line trench. All but two of the burials belong to these battalions.

Devonshire Cemetery contains 163 Commonwealth burials of the First World War, ten of which are unidentified.

The cemetery was designed by W H Cowlishaw.

YPRES (MENIN GATE) MEMORIAL

Country: Belgium
Locality: Ieper, West-Vlaanderen
Identified casualties: 54,405

Location information

Ypres (now Ieper) is a town in the province of West Flanders. The memorial is situated at the eastern side of the town on the road to Menin (Menen) and Courtrai (Kortrijk).

Each night at 8pm the traffic is stopped at the Menin Gate while members of the local Fire Brigade sound the Last Post in the roadway under the memorial's arches.

Historical information

The Menin Gate is one of four memorials to the missing in Belgian Flanders that cover the area known as the Ypres Salient. The Salient stretched from Langemarck in the north to the northern edge in Ploegsteert Wood in the south, but varied in area throughout the war.

The Salient was formed during the First Battle of Ypres in October and November 1914, when a small British Expeditionary Force succeeded in securing the town before the onset of winter, pushing the German forces back to the Passchendaele Ridge. The Second Battle of Ypres began in April 1915 when the Germans released poison gas into the Allied lines. The attack forced an Allied withdrawal and a shortening of the line of defence.

There was little more significant activity on this front until 1917, when in the Third Battle of Ypres an offensive was mounted by Commonwealth forces to divert German attention from a weakened French front further south. The initial attempt in June to dislodge the Germans from the

Messines Ridge was a success, but the main assault north-eastward, which began at the end of July, quickly became a dogged struggle in rapidly deteriorating weather. The campaign finally came to a close in November with the capture of Passchendaele. The German offensive of March 1918 met with some initial success, but was eventually stopped in a combined effort by the Allies in September.

The site of the Menin Gate was chosen because of the hundreds of thousands of men who passed through it on their way to the battlefields. It commemorates casualties from the forces of Australia, Canada, India, South Africa and the UK who died in the Salient. In the case of the UK, the casualties are mainly only those from prior to 16th August 1917.

The Ypres (Menin Gate) Memorial now bears the names of more than 54,000 officers and men whose graves are not known. The memorial, designed by Sir Reginald Blomfield with sculpture by Sir William Reid-Dick, was unveiled by Lord Plumer on 24th July 1927.

MERVILLE COMMUNAL CEMETERY

Country: France
Locality: Nord
Identified casualties: 1,262

Location information

Merville is a town 15km north of Bethune and about 20km south west of Armentières. The Communal Cemetery is on the north-east side of the town and to the north of the D38 road to Neuf-Berquin.

Historical information

Merville was the scene of fighting between the Germans, French and British cavalry early in the First World War but, from 9th October 1914 to 11th April 1918, it remained in Allied hands. In October 1914, and in the autumn of 1915, the town was the headquarters of the Indian Corps. It was a railhead until May 1915, and a billeting and hospital centre from 1915–18. The 6th and Lahore Casualty Clearing Stations were there from the autumn of 1914 to the autumn of 1915; the 7th from December 1914 to April 1917; the 54th (1st/2nd London) from August 1915 to March 1918, and the 51st (Highland) from May 1917 to April 1918.

On the evening of 11th April 1918, in the Battles of the Lys, the Germans forced their way into Merville and the town was not retaken until 19th August. The cemeteries were not used again until the concentration of battlefield burials into the Extension began, after the Armistice.

MONTREUIL-AUX-LIONS BRITISH CEMETERY

Country: France
Locality: Aisne
Identified casualties: 75

Location information

Montreuil-Aux-Lions is a commune 17km west of Chateau Thierry. Montreuil-Aux-Lions British Cemetery is a small cemetery set on the side of a main road. It is situated to the east of the village of Montreuil-Aux-Lions.

The cemetery can be reached from the direction of Chateau Thierry, following the N3 Chateau Thierry to La Ferté-sous-Jouarre road. On leaving Chateau Thierry via the N3, the road continues through several hamlets. After about 20km, the road starts to descend into the village of Montreuil-Aux-Lions, and at this point the cemetery is visible on the left side of the road.

Alternatively, the cemetery can be reached from the A4 motorway at the junction for Meaux and La Ferté-sous-Jouarre by following the N3 road to the centre of the town of La Ferté-sous-Jouarre. The second exit should be taken at the roundabout, with a war memorial on the right side of the road, and then continue over a bridge and out of the town of La Ferté-sous-Jouarre, still following the N3 road to Chateau Thierry. After about 10km you will pass through the village of Montreuil-Aux-Lions and on exiting the village the cemetery is visible on the right side of the road.

Historical information

The cemetery was built after the Armistice, when graves were brought in from the battlefields of the Aisne. In addition, a number of graves were brought in during the 1930s from the following surrounding smaller sites:

Branges Churchyard, Chacrise Communal Cemetery, Chateau-Thierry Communal Cemetery, Coulonges-en-Tardenois Communal Cemetery, Coyolles Communal Cemetery, Dhuisy Communal Cemetery, Largny Churchyard, Latilly Communal Cemetery, Louâtre Churchyard, Puiseux Communal Cemetery, Rozay-en-Brie Communal Cemetery, Sommelans Churchyard and Veuilly-la-Poterie Communal Cemetery.

The cemetery contains 171 Commonwealth burials and commemorations of the First World War. 102 of the burials are unidentified, but there are special memorials to 16 casualties known or believed to be buried among them; in the case of eight men of the 1st Dorset, the special memorial is a panel behind the Cross of Sacrifice.

BAGHDAD (NORTH GATE) WAR CEMETERY

Country: Iraq
Identified casualties: 4,454

Location information

Baghdad (North Gate) War Cemetery is located in a very sensitive area in the Waziriah area of the Al-Russafa district of Baghdad. The main entrance to the cemetery is located opposite

the College of Arts and the Institute of Administration in Baghdad University, and adjacent to the Iraqi Cigarette Factory in Waziriah Area.

Visiting information

Whilst the current climate of political instability persists it is not possible for the Commission to manage or maintain its cemeteries and memorials located within Iraq. Alternative arrangements for commemoration have therefore been implemented and a two-volume Roll of Honour listing all casualties buried and commemorated in Iraq has been produced. These volumes are on display at the Commission's Head Office in Maidenhead and are available for the public to view.

Historical information

In 1914, Baghdad was the headquarters of the Turkish Army in Mesopotamia. It was the ultimate objective of the Indian Expeditionary Force 'D' and the goal of the force besieged and captured at Kut in 1916. The city finally fell in March 1917 but, the position was not fully consolidated until the end of April. Nevertheless, it had by that time become the Expeditionary Force's advanced base, with two stationary hospitals and three casualty clearing stations.

The North Gate Cemetery was begun in April 1917 and has been greatly enlarged since the end of the First World War by graves brought in from other burial grounds in Baghdad and northern Iraq, and from battlefields and cemeteries in Anatolia where Commonwealth prisoners of war were buried by the Turks.

At present, 4,160 Commonwealth casualties of the First World War are commemorated by name in the cemetery, many of them on special memorials. Unidentified burials from this period number 2,729.

The cemetery also contains the grave of Lieutenant General Sir Stanley Maude, Commander-in-Chief of the Mesopotamian Expeditionary Force, who died at Baghdad in November 1917, and the memorial to the 13th Division which he commanded.

PLOEGSTEERT MEMORIAL

Country: Belgium

Locality: Comines-Warneton, Hainaut

Identified casualties: 11,383

Location information

The Ploegsteert Memorial stands in Berks Cemetery Extension, which is located 12.5km south of Ieper town centre, on the N365 leading from Ieper to Mesen (Messines), Ploegsteert and on to Armentières.

From Ieper town centre the Rijselsestraat runs from the market square, through the Lille Gate (Rijselpoort) and directly over the crossroads with the Ieper ring road. The road name then changes to the Rijselseweg (N336). 3.5km along the N336 lies a fork junction with the N365. The N365, which forms the right-hand fork, leads to the town of Mesen. The cemetery lies 3km beyond Mesen on the right-hand side of the N365, and opposite Hyde Park Corner (Royal Berks) Cemetery.

Historical information

The Ploegsteert Memorial commemorates more than 11,000 servicemen of the UK and South Africa who died in this sector during the First World War and have no known grave. The memorial serves the area from the line Caestre-Dranoutre-Warneton to the north, to Haverskerque-Estaires-Fournes to the south, including the towns of Hazebrouck, Merville, Bailleul and Armentières, the Forest of Nieppe, and Ploegsteert Wood. The original intention had been to erect the memorial in Lille.

Most of those commemorated by the memorial did not die in major offensives. Most were killed in the course of the day-to-day trench warfare, or in small scale set engagements, usually carried out in support of the major attacks taking place elsewhere.

Berks Cemetery Extension, in which the memorial stands, was begun in June 1916 and used continuously until September 1917. At the Armistice, the extension comprised Plot I only, but Plots II and III were added in 1930 when graves were brought in from Rosenberg Chateau Military Cemetery and Extension, about 1km to the north west. Rosenberg Chateau Military Cemetery was used by fighting units from November 1914 to August 1916. The extension was begun in May 1916 and used until March 1918. Together, the Rosenberg Chateau cemetery and extension were sometimes referred to as 'Red Lodge'. Berks Cemetery Extension now contains 876 First World War burials.

Hyde Park Corner (Royal Berks) Cemetery is separated from Berks Cemetery Extension by a road. It was begun in April 1915 by the 1st/4th Royal Berkshire Regiment and was used at intervals until November 1917. Hyde Park Corner was a road junction to the north of Ploegsteert Wood. Hill 63 was to the north west and nearby were the 'Catacombs', deep shelters capable of holding two battalions, which were used from November 1916 onwards.

The cemetery contains 83 Commonwealth burials of the First World War and four German war graves.

The cemetery, cemetery extension and memorial were designed by Harold Chalton Bradshaw, with sculpture by Gilbert Ledward. The memorial was unveiled by the Duke of Brabant on 7th June 1931.

POZIERES MEMORIAL

Country: France
Locality: Somme
Identified casualties: 14,657

Location information

Pozières is a village 6km north east of the town of Albert. The memorial encloses Pozières British Cemetery, which is south

west of the village on the north side of the main road, D929, from Albert to Pozières.

On the road frontage is an open arcade terminated by small buildings and broken in the middle by the entrance and gates. Along the sides and the back, stone tablets are fixed in the stone rubble walls bearing the names of the dead grouped under their regiments.

It should be added that, although the memorial stands in a cemetery of largely Australian graves, it does not bear any Australian names. The Australian soldiers who fell in France and whose graves are not known are commemorated on the National Memorial at Villers-Bretonneux.

Historical information

The Pozières Memorial relates to the period of crisis in March and April 1918 when the Allied Fifth Army was driven back by overwhelming numbers across the former Somme battlefields, and the months that followed before the Advance to Victory, which began on 8th August 1918.

The memorial commemorates over 14,000 casualties of the UK, and 300 of the South African forces, who have no known grave and who died on the Somme between 21st March and 7th August 1918. The corps and regiments most largely represented are The Rifle Brigade with over 600 names, The Durham Light Infantry with approximately 600 names, The Machine Gun Corps with over 500, The Manchester Regiment with approximately 500 and The Royal Horse and Royal Field Artillery with over 400 names.

The memorial encloses Pozières British Cemetery, Plot II of which contains original burials of 1916, 1917 and 1918, carried out by fighting units and field ambulances. The remaining plots were made after the Armistice when graves were brought in from the battlefields immediately surrounding the cemetery, the majority of them of soldiers who died in the autumn of 1916 during the latter stages of the Battle of the Somme, but a few represent the fighting in August 1918.

There are now 2,758 Commonwealth servicemen buried or commemorated in this cemetery. 1,380 of the burials are unidentified but there are special memorials to 23 casualties known or believed to be buried among them. There is also one German soldier buried here.

The cemetery and memorial were designed by WH Cowlishaw, with sculpture by Laurence A Turner. The memorial was unveiled by Sir Horace Smith-Dorrien on 4 August 1930.

RAMLEH WAR CEMETERY

Country: Israel and Palestine (including Gaza)

Identified casualties: 3,502

Location information

From Tel Aviv, take road number one (Ayalon) south towards Jerusalem. Leave at the exit signposted Lod/Ramleh. This is the exit after Ben Gurion Airport. Proceed along Route 40 for approximately 5km. At the traffic lights signposted Lod (south), turn right. At the roundabout turn left. The cemetery entrance is on the left, after 400m.

Historical information

The cemetery dates from the First World War, when Ramleh (now Ramla) was occupied by the 1st Australian Light Horse Brigade on 1st November 1917. Field ambulances, and later casualty clearing stations, were posted at Ramleh and Lydda from December 1917 onwards. The cemetery was started by the medical units but some graves were brought in later from the battlefields and from Latron, Sarona, Wilhema Military and Indian cemeteries.

During the Second World War, Ramleh War Cemetery was used by the Ramla Royal Air Force Station and by various Commonwealth hospitals posted to the area over the conflict.

Ramleh War Cemetery contains 3,300 Commonwealth burials from the First World War, 964 of them unidentified. Second World War burials number 1,168. There are also 891 war graves of other nationalities from both wars, and 525 non-war burials, many from the RAF and garrison stations that were at Ramleh in the inter-war years, and until the end of the British Mandate for Palestine in 1948.

Within Ramleh War Cemetery will be found the Ramleh 1914– 18 Memorial, erected in 1961 to commemorate more than 300 Commonwealth, German and Turkish servicemen of the First World War who lie buried in cemeteries elsewhere in Israel and where their graves could no longer be maintained. Only 74 of the casualties are named.

HASLAR ROYAL NAVAL CEMETERY

Country: United Kingdom
Locality: Hampshire
Identified casualties: 1,347

Visiting information

A visitor information panel has recently been installed at Haslar Royal Naval Cemetery to provide information about the war casualties buried there.

The cemetery is open at all times. The large main gate is sometimes locked to restrict vehicle access, but the small wooden gate is always open.

Historical information

During both wars, Gosport was a significant seaport and Naval depot, with many government factories and installations based there, as well as the Haslar Naval Hospital. No 5 Squadron Royal Flying Corps were based at Gosport just before the outbreak of the First World War and during the Second World War the town acted as base to No 17 Group Royal Air Force and the Royal Navy Light Coastal Forces.

Haslar Royal Naval Cemetery, which was attached to the Naval Hospital of 2,000 beds, contains 772 First World War graves, two of which are unidentified. Most of the graves are scattered throughout the cemetery, but the 42 officers and men of HM Submarine L.55, whose bodies were brought back from the Baltic in 1928, lie together in a collective grave and their names appear on a screen wall memorial.

SOISSONS MEMORIAL

Country: France
Locality: Aisne
Identified casualties: 3,876

Location information

The town of Soissons stands on the left bank of the River Aisne, approximately 100km north east of Paris.

From RN2 (Soissons bypass coming from Paris/Meaux/Compiegne/Rouen or from Laon):

Exit the RN2 dual carriageway at the Reims exit and turn right (coming from Laon) or turn left (coming from Paris/Meaux/Compiegne/Rouen) at the traffic lights and head into the town. After crossing the railway bridge, bear left onto Rue de Villeneuve, keeping the railway marshalling yards to your left, to arrive at Soissons Railway Station.

From Soissons Railway Station by foot/car:

At the railway station traffic lights turn right onto the Avenue du General de Gaulle in the direction of 'Centre Ville' to the large roundabout (Place de la Republique). Take the second exit marked Centre Ville and bear right into the main street, Rue St Martin which is one-way. Continue along the Rue St Martin until you see the Post Office (La Poste) on the right and then take the side road on the right, Rue du Mont Revers, also one-way, immediately after the small chapel-style building.

The Soissons Memorial is situated to the rear of this building and is easily identifiable by its massive white Portland stone construction. There is parking available on the adjacent streets.

Historical information

The original British Expeditionary Force crossed the Aisne in August 1914 a few kilometres west of Soissons, and re-crossed the river in September a few kilometres east. For the next three and a half years, this part of the front was held by French forces and the city remained within the range of German artillery.

At the end of April 1918, five divisions of Commonwealth forces (IX Corps) were posted to the French 6th Army in this sector to rest and refit following the German offensives on the Somme and Lys. Here, at the end of May, they found themselves facing the overwhelming German attack which, despite fierce opposition, pushed the Allies back across the Aisne to the Marne. Having suffered 15,000 fatal casualties, IX Corps was withdrawn from this front in early July but, was replaced by XXII Corps, who took part in the Allied counter attack that drove back the Germans by early August and recovered the lost ground.

The Soissons Memorial commemorates almost 4,000 officers and men of the United Kingdom forces who died during the Battles of the Aisne and the Marne in 1918 and who have no known grave.

The memorial was designed by GH Holt and VO Rees, with sculpture by Eric Kennington. It was unveiled by Sir Alexander Hamilton-Gordon on 22nd July 1928.

SUCRERIE CEMETERY, EPINOY

Country: France

Locality: Pas de Calais

Identified casualties: 95

Location information

Epinoy is a small village on the N43 road between Cambrai and Douai, some 8km north west of Cambrai itself. Sucrerie Cemetery is located 1km further north along the N43 from Epinoy.

Historical information

Epinoy was captured by the 11th (Northern) Division on 27th September 1918 and the cemetery was made by fighting units after the battle.

The cemetery contains 100 burials and commemorations of the First World War (mainly 6th York and Lancasters, 5th Dorsets and 11th Manchesters). Five of the burials are unidentified but there is a special memorial to one soldier believed to be buried in one of them.

The cemetery was designed by WC Von Berg.

THIEPVAL MEMORIAL

Country: France

Locality: Somme

Identified casualties: 72,195

Location information

The Thiepval Memorial is found on the D73, next to the village of Thiepval, off the main Bapaume to Albert road (D929).

Historical information

On 1st July 1916, supported by a French attack to the south, 13 divisions of Commonwealth forces launched an offensive on a line from north of Gommecourt to Maricourt. Despite a preliminary bombardment lasting seven days, the German defences were barely touched and the attack met unexpectedly fierce resistance. Losses were catastrophic and, with only minimal advances on the southern flank, the initial attack was a failure. In the following weeks, huge resources of manpower and equipment were deployed in an attempt to exploit the modest successes of the first day. However, the German Army resisted and repeated attacks and counter attacks meant a major battle for every village, copse and farmhouse gained. At the end of September, Thiepval was finally captured. The village had been an original objective of 1st July. Attacks north and east continued throughout October and into November in increasingly difficult weather conditions. The Battle of the Somme finally ended on 18th November with the onset of winter.

In the spring of 1917, the German forces fell back to their newly prepared defences, the Hindenburg Line, and there were no further significant engagements in the Somme sector until the Germans mounted their major offensive in March 1918.

The Thiepval Memorial – the Memorial to the Missing of the Somme – bears the names of more than 72,000 officers and men of the UK and South African forces who died in the Somme sector before 20th March 1918 and have no known grave. Over 90% of those commemorated died between July and November 1916. The memorial also serves as an Anglo-French Battle Memorial in recognition of the joint nature of the 1916 offensive and a small cemetery containing equal numbers of Commonwealth and French graves lies at the foot of the memorial.

The memorial, designed by Sir Edwin Lutyens, was built between 1928 and 1932 and unveiled by HRH the Prince of Wales, in the presence of the President of France, on 1st August 1932. It was originally scheduled for 16th May but due to the death of French President Doumer, the ceremony was postponed. Each year a major ceremony is held at the memorial on 1st July.

The dead of other Commonwealth countries, who died on the Somme and have no known graves, are commemorated on national memorials elsewhere.

THEUX COMMUNAL CEMETERY

Country:	Belgium
Locality:	Theux, Liege
Identified casualties:	31

Location information

The village of Theux is located south west of the town of Verviers on the N62. From the motorway E40, which runs between Brussels and Aachen, turn off at the junction with the E42 and follow the E42 direction Verviers. Turn off the E42 at junction 8 and onto the N657, direction Theux, and  follow this road to the junction with the N690. In the village centre turn right by the town hall into Rue De La Chaussée to the junction with the N62. Turn right in the direction of Louveigné along Rue Tillot. The cemetery is along on the left after the sharp left-hand bend. The graves are located along the right-hand side of the cemetery, halfway along.

Historical information

The 36th Clearing Station was posted to the village of Theux from December 1918 to January 1919, and the 61st from January to April 1919.

Theux Communal Cemetery contains 31 Commonwealth burials from the First World War.

TYNE COT MEMORIAL

Country:	Belgium
Locality:	Zonnebeke, West-Vlaanderen
Identified casualties:	34,948

Location information

The Tyne Cot Memorial to the Missing forms the north-eastern boundary of Tyne Cot Cemetery, which is located 9km north east of Ieper town centre, on the Tynecotstraat, a road leading from the Zonnebeekseweg (N332).

The names of those from UK units are inscribed on panels arranged by regiment, under their respective ranks. The names of those from New Zealand units are inscribed on panels within the New Zealand Memorial Apse located at the centre of the memorial.

Historical information

The Tyne Cot Memorial is one of four memorials to the missing in Belgian Flanders, which covers the area known as the Ypres Salient. Broadly speaking, the Salient stretched from Langemarck in the north to the northern edge in Ploegsteert Wood in the south, but it varied in area and shape throughout the war.

The Salient was formed during the First Battle of Ypres in October and November 1914, when a small British expeditionary force succeeded in securing the town before the onset of winter, pushing the German forces back to the Passchendaele Ridge. The Second Battle of Ypres began in April 1915 when the Germans released poison gas into the Allied lines north of Ypres.

There was little more significant activity on this front until 1917 when, in the Third Battle of Ypres, an offensive was mounted by Commonwealth forces to divert German attention from a weakened French front further south. The initial attempt in June to dislodge the Germans from the Messines Ridge was a success, but the main assault north-eastward, which began at the end of July, quickly became a dogged struggle against determined opposition and the rapidly deteriorating weather.

The campaign finally came to a close in November with the capture of Passchendaele.

The German offensive of March 1918 met with some initial success, but was eventually checked in a combined effort by the Allies in September.

The battles of the Ypres Salient claimed many lives on both sides and it quickly became clear that the commemoration of members of the Commonwealth forces with no known grave would have to be divided between several different sites.

The site of the Menin Gate was chosen because of the hundreds of thousands of men who passed through it on their way to the battlefields. It commemorates those of all Commonwealth nations, except New Zealand, who died in the Salient, in the case of UK casualties before 16 August 1917 (with some exceptions). Those United Kingdom and New Zealand servicemen who died after that date are named on the memorial at Tyne Cot, a site which marks the furthest point reached by Commonwealth forces in Belgium until nearly the end of the war.

The Tyne Cot Memorial now bears the names of almost 35,000 officers and men whose graves are not known. The memorial, designed by Sir Herbert Baker with sculpture by Joseph Armitage and FV Blundstone, was unveiled by Sir Gilbert Dyett on 20 June 1927.

The memorial forms the north-eastern boundary of Tyne Cot Cemetery, which was established around a captured German blockhouse or pill-box used as an advanced dressing station. The original battlefield cemetery of 343 graves was greatly enlarged after the Armistice when remains were brought in from the battlefields of Passchendaele and Langemarck, and from a few small burial grounds. It is now the largest Commonwealth war cemetery in the world in terms of burials. At the suggestion of His Majesty King George V, who visited the cemetery in 1922, the Cross of Sacrifice was placed on the original large pill-box. There are three other pill-boxes in the cemetery.

There are now 11,956 Commonwealth servicemen of the First World War buried or commemorated in Tyne Cot Cemetery, 8,369 of these are unidentified.

The cemetery was designed by Sir Herbert Baker.

VIMY MEMORIAL

Country: France

Locality: Pas de Calais

Identified casualties: 11,168

Location information

The Vimy Memorial overlooks the Douai Plain from the highest point of Vimy Ridge, about 8km north east of Arras on the N17 towards Lens. The memorial is signposted from this road to the left, just before you enter the village of Vimy from the south. The memorial itself is some way inside the memorial park, but again it is well signposted.

Historical information

On the opening day of the Battle of Arras, 9th April 1917, the four divisions of the Canadian Corps, fighting side by side for the first time, scored a huge tactical victory in the capture of the 60m-high Vimy Ridge.

After the war, the highest point of the ridge was chosen as the site of the great memorial to all Canadians who served their country in battle during the First World War, and particularly to the 60,000 who gave their lives in France. It bears the names of 11,000 Canadian servicemen who died in France – many of them in the fight for Vimy Ridge – who have no known grave.

The memorial was designed by WS Allward. It was unveiled by HM King Edward VIII on 26th July 1936.

VIS-EN-ARTOIS MEMORIAL

Country: France
Locality: Pas de Calais
Identified casualties: 9,833

Location information

Vis-en-Artois and Haucourt are villages on the straight main road from Arras to Cambrai, about 10km south-east of Arras.

The memorial is the back drop to the Vis-en-Artois British Cemetery, which is west of Haucourt on the north side of the main road.

Historical information

This memorial bears the names of over 9,000 men who fell in the period from 8th August 1918 to the date of the Armistice in the Advance to Victory in Picardy and Artois, and who have no known grave. They belonged to the forces of Great Britain, Ireland and South Africa; the Canadian, Australian and New Zealand forces being commemorated on other memorials to the missing.

The memorial consists of a screen wall in three parts. The middle part of the screen wall is concave and carries stone panels on which the names are carved. It is 26ft high, flanked by pylons 70ft high. The Stone of Remembrance stands exactly between the pylons and behind, in the middle of the screen, is a group in relief representing St George and the Dragon. The flanking parts of the screen wall are also curved and carry stone panels carved with names. Each of them forms the back of a roofed colonnade; and at the far end of each is a small building.

The Vis-en-Artois Memorial was designed by JR Truelove, with sculpture by Ernest Gillick. It was unveiled by the Rt Hon Thomas Shaw on 4th August 1930.

WANCOURT BRITISH CEMETERY

Country: France
Locality: Pas de Calais
Identified casualties: 1,107

Location information

Wancourt is a village about 8km south east of Arras. It is 2km south of the main road from Arras to Cambrai. The cemetery is a short distance south east of the village, just off the D35 road.

Historical information

Wancourt was captured on 12th April 1917 after very heavy fighting, and the advance was continued on the following days. The cemetery, called at first Cojeul Valley Cemetery, or River Road Cemetery, was opened about 10 days later. It was used until October 1918 but, was in German hands from March 1918 until 26th August, when the Canadian Corps recaptured Wancourt.

At the Armistice, the cemetery contained 410 graves but was greatly increased in the following years when the fallen were brought in from the following small cemeteries and isolated positions on the battlefields south east of Arras:

St Martin-Croisilles Road Cemetery, in the commune of St Martin-sur-Cojeul. In this graveyard, about midway along the road, were buried 15 British officers and men who fell on 9th April 1917, or the four following days, and of whom 13 belonged to the 1st East Yorkshire Regiment.

Shaft Trench Cemetery, in the commune of Heninel, about 1,600m from that village on the road to Croisilles. Here, in April, May and June 1917, 19 British soldiers were buried by the 50th (Northumbrian) Division.

Signal Trench Cemetery, Heninel. Here, on the far side of the ridge between Wancourt and Cherisy, 'in a rather broken part of the British front line', 22 British soldiers were buried in April and May 1917.

Fontaine Road Cemetery, Heninel. In this graveyard, slightly north of Signal Trench Cemetery, 17 British officers and men (of whom 15 belonged to the 2nd Royal Welch Fusiliers) were buried in April 1917.

Heninel-Cherisy Road West Cemetery, Heninel, which was about 800m east of Heninel village, contained 25 British graves from April 1917.

The Lincolns Cemetery, St Martin-sur-Cojeul, about 800m south east of that village, where 22 non-commissioned officers and men of the 1st Lincolns, who fell on 11th April 1917, were buried.

Henin North Cemetery, Henin-sur-Cojeul, about 800m north of the village, contained the graves of 29 British soldiers killed on 9th April 1917, almost all of whom belonged to the 2nd Wilts or the 18th King's Liverpools.

The Wancourt Cemetery now contains 1,936 burials and commemorations from the First World War. Although 829 of the burials are unidentified, there are special memorials to 76 casualties known or believed to be buried among them, and to 20 who were buried in Signal Trench Cemetery whose graves were destroyed in later battles.

Wancourt Cemetery was designed by Sir Edwin Lutyens.

WEYMOUTH CEMETERY

Country: United Kingdom

Locality: Dorset

Identified casualties: 77

Historical information

During the two world wars, the UK became an island fortress used for training troops and launching land, sea and air operations around the globe. There are more than 170,000 Commonwealth war graves in the UK, many being those of servicemen and women killed on active service, or who later succumbed to wounds. Others died in training accidents, or because of sickness or disease. The graves, many of them privately owned and marked by private memorials, will be found in more than 12,000 cemeteries and churchyards.

Weymouth Cemetery contains 62 burials relating to the First World War and 15 from the Second World War, all in different parts of the cemetery.

WORLD WAR I AND WORLD WAR II

BROOKWOOD MEMORIAL

Country:	United Kingdom
Locality:	Surrey
Identified casualties:	320

Location information

Brookwood is 30 miles from London (take the M3 to Bagshot and then the A322). The main entrance to Brookwood Military Cemetery is on the A324 from the village of Pirbright. There is a direct train service from Waterloo to Brookwood Station, from which there is an entrance to the cemetery.

The United Kingdom 1914–18 Memorial stands at the north-eastern end of the 1914–18 Plot.

Historical information

Brookwood Military Cemetery is owned by the War Graves Commission and is the largest Commonwealth war cemetery in the UK, covering approximately 37 acres.

In 1917, an area of land in Brookwood Cemetery (The London Necropolis) was set aside for burials of men and women of the forces of the Commonwealth, and Americans, who had died, many of battle wounds, in the London district.

This site was further extended to accommodate the Commonwealth casualties of the Second World War. There is a large Royal Air Forces section in the south-east corner of the cemetery, which also contains the graves of Czech and American airmen who served with the Royal Air Force, and the Air Forces shelter building nearby houses the register of the names of those buried in the section. A plot in the west corner of the cemetery contains approximately 2,400 Canadian graves from the Second World War, including those of 43 men who died of wounds following the Dieppe Raid in August 1942. The Canadian Records building, which was a gift of the Canadian government, houses a reception room for visitors and other offices.

In addition to the Commonwealth plots, the cemetery also contains French, Polish, Czech, Belgian and Italian sections, and a number of war graves of other nationalities, all cared for by the Commission. The American Military Cemetery is the responsibility of the American Battle Monuments Commission.

Brookwood Military Cemetery now contains 1,601 Commonwealth burials relating to the First World War and 3,476 from the Second World War. Of the Second World War burials, five are unidentified; three having been members of the RAF and two of the RCAF.

The war graves of other nationalities in the Commission's care number 786, including 28 unidentified French personnel.

The Brookwood (United Kingdom 1914–18) Memorial was created in 2004. It currently commemorates around 500 Commonwealth casualties who died in the UK during the First World War but for whom no graves could be found. Please note: many of the casualties commemorated by this memorial were only recently notified to, and accepted for commemoration by, the Commission. Therefore, it may not be possible to view all names on this memorial yet. There are also names engraved here where the burial place has since been discovered. Their commemoration details are now recorded correctly under the appropriate cemetery register.

The Brookwood Memorial stands at the southern end of the Canadian section of the cemetery and commemorates 3,500 men and women of the land forces of the Commonwealth who died during the Second

World War and have no known grave. The circumstances of their death meant that they could not appropriately be commemorated on any of the campaign memorials in the various theatres of war. They died in the campaign in Norway in 1940, or in the various raids on enemy occupied territory in Europe such as Dieppe and St Nazaire. Others were special agents who died as prisoners or while working with Allied underground movements. Some died at sea, in hospital ships and troop transports, in waters not associated with the major campaigns, and a few were killed in flying accidents or in aerial combat.

CHATHAM NAVAL MEMORIAL

Country: United Kingdom
Locality: Kent
Identified casualties: 18,625

Location information

From the Brompton Barracks – Chatham: at the traffic signals turn right onto Globe Lane, A231 (signposted 'Historic Dockyards'). Keep in left-hand lane then turn left onto Dock Road (signposted Gillingham). At roundabout take the 2nd exit onto Wood Street, A231 (signposted Gillingham). Turn right on Mansion Row (the memorial is signposted from here), then 1st left on Sally Port Gardens and finally 1st right on King's Bastion. Follow the road through the housing estate. The car park to the memorial is at the end of this road.

The memorial overlooks the town of Chatham and is approached by a steep path from the Town Hall Gardens.

A copy of the Memorial Register is kept in the Naval Chapel of Brompton Garrison Church and may be examined there. The keys to the church are held at the Gate House, which is always manned.

Historical information

After the First World War, an appropriate way had to be found of remembering those of the Royal Navy who had no known grave, the majority of deaths having occurred at sea where no permanent memorial could be provided.

An Admiralty committee recommended that the three manning ports in Great Britain – Chatham, Plymouth and Portsmouth – should each have an identical memorial of unmistakable naval form – an obelisk – which would serve as a leading mark for shipping. The memorials were designed by Sir Robert Lorimer, who had already carried out a considerable amount of work for the Commission, with sculpture by Henry Poole. The Chatham Naval Memorial was unveiled by HRH the Prince of Wales (the future King Edward VIII) on 26th April 1924.

After the Second World War it was decided that the naval memorials should be extended to provide space for commemorating the naval dead without graves of that war, but since the three sites were dissimilar, a different architectural treatment was required for each. The architect for the Second World War extension at Chatham was Sir Edward Maufe, (who also designed the Air Forces memorial at Runnymede), and the additional sculpture was by Charles Wheeler and William McMillan. The extension was unveiled by HRH the Duke of Edinburgh on 15 October 1952.

Chatham Naval Memorial commemorates 8,517 sailors of the First World War and 10,098 of the Second World War.

WORLD WAR II

LEE-ON-SOLENT MEMORIAL

Country:	United Kingdom
Locality:	Hampshire
Identified casualties:	1,926

Location information

This memorial can be found on the main seafront, sited on Marine Parade West, approximately half a mile west of the town centre.

Historical information

During the Second World War the Fleet Air Arm served in almost every theatre. In a reconnaissance role they supported land operations in France, the Netherlands, North Africa, Italy, and the Far East. Operating from aircraft carriers (seven of which were lost during the war), they formed one of the chief weapons against the U-boats in the Atlantic and in support of the Russian convoys.

In November 1940, Fleet Air Arm Swordfish biplanes carrying torpedoes, undertook a night raid on the harbour at Taranto, resulting in disaster for the Italian navy. Aircraft from HMS *Victorious* and *Ark Royal* took part in the sinking of the German battleship *Bismarck* in May 1941 and in February 1942, when the *Scharnhorst*, *Gneisenau* and *Prinz Eugen* attempted a daring dash along the English Channel from the Atlantic to the relative safety of the North Sea, they were attacked by Swordfish of the Fleet Air Arm.

The principal base of the Fleet Air Arm, Lee-on-the-Solent, Hampshire, was chosen as the site for the memorial to almost 2,000 naval men who died during the Second World War and who have no known grave.

PORTSMOUTH NAVAL MEMORIAL

Country: United Kingdom

Locality: Hampshire

Identified casualties: 24,599

Location information

The memorial is situated on Southsea Common overlooking the promenade and, is accessible at all times. A copy of the Memorial Register is kept at the Civic Offices in Guildhall Square, Portsmouth and may be consulted there.

Historical information

After the First World War, an appropriate way had to be found of commemorating those members of the Royal Navy who had no known resting place; the majority of deaths having occurred at sea where no permanent memorial could be provided.

An Admiralty committee recommended that the three manning ports in Great Britain – Chatham, Plymouth and Portsmouth – should each have an identical memorial of unmistakable naval form – an obelisk – which would serve as a leading mark for shipping. The memorials were designed by Sir Robert Lorimer, who had already carried out a considerable amount of work for the Commission, with sculpture by Henry Poole. The Portsmouth Naval Memorial was unveiled by HRH the Duke of York (the future George VI) on 15 October 1924.

After the Second World War it was decided that the naval memorials should be extended to provide space for commemorating the naval dead without graves of that war, but since the three sites were dissimilar, a different architectural treatment was required for each. The architect for the Second World War extension at Portsmouth was Sir Edward Maufe (who also designed the Air Forces memorial at Runnymede) and the additional sculpture was by Charles Wheeler, William McMillan, and Esmond Burton. The extension was unveiled by Queen Elizabeth, the Queen Mother, on 29 April 1953.

Portsmouth Naval Memorial commemorates around 10,000 sailors of the First World War and almost 15,000 of the Second World War.

RUNNYMEDE MEMORIAL

Country: United Kingdom

Locality: Surrey

Identified casualties: 20,323

Location information

This memorial overlooks the River Thames on Cooper's Hill at Englefield Green and is between Windsor and Egham on the A308, 4 miles from Windsor.

Historical information

The Air Forces Memorial at Runnymede commemorates over 20,000 airmen by name who were lost in the Second World War during operations from bases in the UK and Northern and Western Europe, and who have no known graves. They served in Bomber, Fighter, Coastal, Transport, Flying Training and Maintenance Commands, and came from all parts of the Commonwealth. Some were from countries in continental Europe that had been overrun but whose airmen continued to fight in the ranks of the Royal Air Force.

The memorial was designed by Sir Edward Maufe with sculpture by Vernon Hill. The engraved glass and painted ceilings were designed by John Hutton and the poem engraved on the gallery window was written by Paul H Scott. The Memorial was unveiled by HM The Queen on 17 October 1953.

ALAMEIN MEMORIAL

Country: Egypt
Identified casualties: 11,866

Location information

Alamein is a village bypassed by the main coast road, approximately 130km west of Alexandria on the road to Mersa Matruh. The first Commission road-direction sign is located just beyond the Alamein police checkpoint and all cemetery visitors should turn off from the main road onto the parallel old coast road.

The cemetery lies off the road beyond the ridge, and road direction signs are in place approximately 25m before the low metal gates and stone wing walls, which are situated centrally at the road edge at the head of the access path into the cemetery. The Cross of Sacrifice feature may be seen from the road.

Historical information

The campaign in the Western Desert was fought between the Commonwealth forces (with later, the addition of two brigades of Free French and one each of Polish and Greek troops) all based in Egypt, and the Axis forces (German and Italian) based in Libya. The battlefield, across which the fighting surged back and forth between 1940 and 1942, was the 1,000km of desert between Alexandria in Egypt and Benghazi in Libya. It was a campaign of manoeuvre and movement, the objectives being the control of the Mediterranean, the link with the east through the Suez Canal, the Middle East oil supplies and the supply route to Russia through Persia.

The Alamein Memorial forms the entrance to Alamein War Cemetery. The Land Forces panels commemorate more than 8,500 soldiers of the

Commonwealth who died in the campaigns in Egypt and Libya, and in the operations of the Eighth Army in Tunisia up to 19th February 1943, who have no known grave. It also remembers those who served and died in Syria, Lebanon, Iraq and Persia.

The Air Forces panels commemorate more than 3,000 airmen of the Commonwealth who died in the campaigns in Egypt, Libya, Syria, Lebanon, Iraq, Greece, Crete and the Aegean, Ethiopia, Eritrea and the Somalilands, the Sudan, East Africa, Aden and Madagascar, who have no known grave. Those who served with the Rhodesian and South African Air Training Scheme and have no known grave are also commemorated here.

The Memorial was designed by Sir Hubert Worthington and unveiled by Field Marshal The Rt Hon Viscount Montgomery of Alamein on 24th October 1954.

El Alamein War Cemetery contains the graves of men who died at all stages of the Western Desert campaigns, and especially those who died in the Battle of El Alamein at the end of October 1942 and in the period immediately before.

The cemetery now contains 7,239 Commonwealth burials relating to the Second World War, of which 814 are unidentified. There are also 102 war graves appertaining to different nationalities.

ANZIO WAR CEMETERY

Country: Italy
Identified casualties: 1,037

Location information

Anzio is a coastal town 70km south of Rome. To reach Anzio take the No 148 Superstrada Motorway, which runs between Rome and Latina. Take the exit for Anzio and follow the signs towards Anzio along the No 207.

The cemetery lies 1km north of Anzio town just off the No 207. As the No 207 approaches Anzio, an Italian Communal Cemetery is visible on a small rise to the left of the road. Turn left and drive up a small rise to a parking area in front of the cemetery entrance. Commission signs are visible.

Anzio War Cemetery should not be confused with Beach Head Cemetery which is also close to Anzio town. Beach Head Cemetery lies on the No 207, 5km north of Anzio town, and can be seen on the left-hand side of the road when taking the No 207 towards Anzio.

Historical information

On 3 September 1943 the Allies invaded the Italian mainland, the invasion coinciding with an armistice made with the Italians who then re-entered the war on the Allied side.

Progress through southern Italy was rapid despite stiff resistance, but by the end of October, the Allies were facing the German winter defensive position known as the Gustav Line, which stretched from the Garigliano river in the west to the Sangro in the east. Initial attempts to breach the western end of the line were unsuccessful. Operations in January 1944 landed troops behind the German lines at Anzio; however, defences were well organised, and a breakthrough was not actually achieved until May.

The site for this cemetery was selected not long after the landings at Anzio and the burials here date from the period immediately following the landings. Anzio War Cemetery contains 1,056 Commonwealth burials of the Second World War.

The cemetery was designed by Louis de Soissons.

ATHENS MEMORIAL

Country: Greece
Identified casualties: 2,870

Location information

Access to the Athens Memorial is through Phaleron War Cemetery.

Phaleron War Cemetery lies a few kilometres to the south east of Athens, at the boundary between old Phaleron district and Alimos-Kalamaki district, on the coast road from Athens to Vouliagmeni.

The easiest way to reach the cemetery is by the coastal tram, which takes about 35 minutes from the terminus at Syntagma Square on Route 5 (Platon) towards Voula. Alight at Pikrodafni, a stop about 100m after the cemetery, from where it can be easily seen. The Athens Memorial stands in the cemetery.

Historical information

The Athens Memorial stands within Phaleron War Cemetery and commemorates nearly 3,000 members of the land forces of the Commonwealth who lost their lives during the campaigns in Greece and Crete in 1941 and 1944–45; in the Dodecanese Islands in 1943–45; and in Yugoslavia in 1943–45, and who have no known grave.

The site of what is now Phaleron War Cemetery was chosen originally by the 4th Division as a burial ground for Commonwealth casualties of the Greek Civil War (December 1944–February 1945). Subsequently, the military authorities, in conjunction with the Greek Government and the Army Graves Service, decided that it would be the most suitable site for a Second World War cemetery for the whole mainland of Greece. The 23rd and 24th Graves Registration Units and the 21st and 22nd Australian War Graves Units worked together to bring in graves of the 1941 campaign from the battlefields, temporary military cemeteries and from various civil cemeteries.

There are now 2,028 Commonwealth servicemen of the Second World War buried or commemorated in this cemetery. Of these, 596 of the burials are unidentified. Special memorials commemorate casualties known to have been interred in certain groups of graves in the cemetery, but whose individual graves cannot be precisely located within these groups. Other special memorials commemorate casualties re-buried in the cemetery from original graves, which, owing to the destruction of local records, could not be identified.

BOLSENA WAR CEMETERY

Country: Italy
Identified casualties: 557

Location information

Bolsena War Cemetery is situated on the eastern side of Lake Bolsena just west of the SS2, between Rome (104km) and Siena (115km). Take the Orte exit from the autostrada A1. Go 30km west towards Viterbo then turn right on to the SS2.

The two nearest towns are Montefiascone, 8km to the south, and Bolsena on the shores of the lake, 7km to the north. The cemetery entrance can be clearly seen from the main road.

Historical information

On 3 September 1943 the Allies invaded the Italian mainland; the invasion coinciding with an armistice made with the Italians who then re-entered the war on the Allied side.

Progress through southern Italy was rapid despite stiff resistance but the advance was checked for some months at the German winter defensive position known as the Gustav Line. The line eventually fell in May 1944 and, as the Germans fell back, Rome was taken by the Allies on 3rd June.

The Germans made their first stand after being driven north of Rome at Bolsena and to the east of Lake Bolsena, there was a tank battle in June 1944 between the 6th South African Armoured Division and the Hermann Goering Panzer Division.

The site for the cemetery was chosen in November 1944, and graves were brought in from the battlefields between Bolsena and Orvieto. Almost one third of those buried at Bolsena were South Africans. In 1947, 42 graves were brought into the cemetery (into Plot 4 Rows G and H) from the Island of Elba.

The cemetery is on the actual site of the first camp occupied by General Alexander's advanced headquarters after the liberation of Rome and it was here that HM King George VI visited General Alexander at the end of July 1944.

Bolsena War Cemetery contains 597 Commonwealth burials of the Second World War, 40 of them unidentified.

The cemetery was designed by Louis de Soissons.

CASSINO WAR CEMETERY

Country: Italy
Identified casualties: 3,982

Location information

Cassino War Cemetery lies in the Commune of Cassino, Province of Frosinone, 139km south east of Rome.

Take the autostrada A1 from Rome to Naples and leave it at the Cassino exit. Take the roundabout and then the third exit and follow the road signs to Cassino. On this road you will find the first of six clearly visible signposts to the cemetery and memorial.

The cemetery is located approximately 1km from the railway station in Via Sant' Angelo and visitors arriving by train are advised to take a taxi from the station.

Historical information

On 3 September 1943 the Allies invaded the Italian mainland, the invasion coinciding with an armistice made with the Italians who then re-entered the war on the Allied side.

Progress through southern Italy was rapid despite stiff resistance but, by the end of October, the Allies were facing the German winter defensive position known as the Gustav Line, which stretched from the river Garigliano in the west to the Sangro in the east. Initial attempts to breach the western end of the line were unsuccessful. Operations in January 1944 landed troops behind the German lines at Anzio, but defences were well organised, and a breakthrough was not actually achieved until 18th May, when Cassino was finally taken.

The site for Cassino War Cemetery was originally selected in January 1944, but the development of the battle during the first five months of that year made it impossible to use until after the Germans had withdrawn from Cassino. During these early months of 1944, Cassino saw some of the fiercest fighting of the Italian campaign; the town itself and the dominating Monastery Hill proving the most stubborn obstacles encountered in the advance towards Rome. The majority of those buried in the war cemetery died in the battles during these months.

There are now 4,271 Commonwealth servicemen of the Second World War buried or commemorated at Cassino War Cemetery. Some 289 of the burials are unidentified.

Within the cemetery stands the Cassino Memorial which commemorates over 4,000 Commonwealth servicemen who took part in the Italian campaign and whose graves are not known.

CATANIA WAR CEMETERY, SICILY

Country: Italy
Locality: Sicily
Identified casualties: 2,022

Location information

Catania War Cemetery is 7km south west of Catania. From Catania Airport follow the tangenziale (main road) towards the A19 (in the direction of Palermo). Before reaching the A19 the cemetery is signposted.

Historical information

On 10 July 1943, following the successful conclusion of the North African campaign in mid- May, a combined allied force of 160,000 Commonwealth and American troops invaded Sicily as a prelude to the assault on mainland Italy. The Italians, who would shortly make peace with the Allies and re-enter the war on their side, offered little determined resistance but German opposition was vigorous and stubborn. The campaign in Sicily came to an end on 17th August when the two allied forces joined at Messina yet failed to cut off the retreating Axis lines.

Catania War Cemetery contains burials from the later stages of the campaign, as it went from Lentini northwards. Many died in the heavy fighting just short of Catania (the town was taken on 5th August) and in the battle for the Simeto river bridgehead.

Catania War Cemetery contains 2,135 Commonwealth burials from the Second World War, 113 of them unidentified.

CESENA WAR CEMETERY

Country: Italy
Identified casualties: 772

Location information

Cesena War Cemetery lies in the Commune of Cesena, in the Province of Forli.

Take the autostrada A14, Bologna–Ancona, exiting at Cesena. Proceed along this road for about 4km, arriving at a roundabout. Turn left and then take the second road on the right. After 50m, turning left, enter into a parking area and take a little road leading to the cemetery main entrance.

Historical information

On 3 September 1943 the Allies invaded the Italian mainland, the invasion coinciding with an armistice made with the Italians who then re-entered the war on the Allied side.

Following the fall of Rome to the Allies in June 1944, the German retreat became ordered and successive stands were made on a series of defensive lines. In the northern Apennine mountains, the last of these, the Gothic Line, was breached by the Allies during the autumn campaign and the front inched forward as far as Ravenna in the Adriatic sector. However, with divisions transferred to support the new offensive in France, and the Germans dug into a number of key defensive positions, the advance stalled as winter set in.

Most of those buried in this cemetery died during the advance from Rimini to Forli and beyond in September–November 1944. It was an advance across one flooded river after another in atrocious autumn weather. The cemetery site was selected in November 1944 and burials were brought in from the surrounding battlefields.

Cesena War Cemetery contains 775 Commonwealth burials of the Second World War.

DURNBACH WAR CEMETERY

Country: Germany

Locality: Bad Tölz, Bayern

Identified casualties: 2,841

Location information

The small village of Durnbach lies in the south of Germany, approximately 45km south of Munich. From the A8 Munich to Salzburg motorway, take exit 97 (Ausfahrt 97) Holzkirchen/ Tegernsee/Bad Wiesee/Bad Tölz and follow the B318 direction Gmund Am Tegernsee. Continue for approximately 14km and then turn left (CWGC sign) onto the B472, direction Miesbach. Continue for approximately 1km and the cemetery can be found on the left.

Historical information

The site for Durnbach War Cemetery was chosen shortly after hostilities had ceased, by officers of the British Army and Air Force, in conjunction with officers of the American occupation forces in whose zone Durnbach lay.

The great majority of those buried there are airmen shot down over Bavaria, Württemberg, Austria, Hessen and Thuringia, brought from their scattered graves by the Army Graves Service. The remainder are men who were killed while escaping from prisoner of war camps in the same areas, or who died towards the end of the war on forced marches from the camps to more remote areas.

Durnbach War Cemetery contains 2,934 Commonwealth burials of the Second World War, 93 of which are unidentified. One grave in the cemetery (III. C. 22.) contains the ashes of an unknown number of unidentified war casualties recovered from Flossenbürg. Also, one grave (IV. A. 21.) contains the remains of six unidentified UK airmen. There are also 30 war graves of other nationalities, most of them Polish.

EL ALAMEIN WAR CEMETERY

Country: Egypt
Identified casualties: 6,425

Location information

Alamein is a village, bypassed by the main coast road, approximately 130km west of Alexandria, on the road to Mersa Matruh.

The first Commission road direction sign is located just beyond the Alamein police checkpoint and all visitors should turn off from the main road onto the parallel old coast road.

The cemetery lies off the road, slightly beyond a ridge, and is indicated by road direction signs approximately 25m before the low metal gates and stone wing walls, which are situated centrally at the road edge at the head of the access path into the cemetery. The Cross of Sacrifice feature may be seen from the road.

Historical information

The campaign in the Western Desert was fought between the Commonwealth forces (with, later, the addition of two brigades of Free French and one each of Polish and Greek troops) all based in Egypt, and the Axis forces (German and Italian) based in Libya. The battlefield, across which the fighting surged back and forth between 1940 and 1942, was the 1,000km of desert between Alexandria in Egypt and Benghazi in Libya. It was a campaign of manoeuvre and movement, the objectives being the control of the Mediterranean, the link with the east through the

Suez Canal, the Middle East oil supplies and the supply route to Russia through Persia.

El Alamein War Cemetery contains the graves of men who died at all stages of the Western Desert campaigns, brought in from a wide area, especially those who died in the Battle of El Alamein at the end of October 1942 and in the period immediately before.

The cemetery now contains 7,240 Commonwealth burials of the Second World War, of which 815 are unidentified. There are also 102 war graves of other nationalities.

EL ALIA CEMETERY

Country: Algeria
Identified casualties: 344

Location information

El Alia Cemetery is approximately 13km south east of Algiers on the road to El Harrach and is situated within a large civilian cemetery. The Commonwealth plot is approximately 400m from the main gate, and is reached by turning left at the end of the central avenue.

Historical information

Allied troops made a series of landings on the Algerian coast in early November 1942. From there, they swept east into Tunisia, where the North African campaign came to an end in May 1943 with the surrender of the Axis forces.

The cemetery was originally an Allied war cemetery, but was taken over as a civilian cemetery by the municipal authorities when most of the non-Commonwealth war graves were moved to other burial places.

El Alia Cemetery now contains 368 Commonwealth burials of the Second World War. Eight war graves of other nationalities remain in the Commonwealth plot and there are also 15 non-war graves, mostly of merchant seamen whose deaths were not due to war service.

IBADAN MILITARY CEMETERY

Country: Nigeria
Identified casualties: 131

Location information

The cemetery is situated in the Jericho district of Ibadan near the Forestry Department Research Centre, 3km from the railway station. The gateway constructed at the entrance to the cemetery is approached by a drive off the main road leading to the Government Rest House. In the centre of the  cemetery stands the Cross of Sacrifice and there are eight denominational plots where the graves are distributed.

Historical information

This cemetery contains the graves of 137 Commonwealth casualties of the Second World War, 6 of which are unidentified. There are 8 foreign national burials and 17 non-world war burials.

REICHSWALD FOREST WAR CEMETERY

Country: Germany
Locality: Kleve, Nordrhein-Westfalen
Identified casualties: 7,418

Location information

The town of Kleve lies in the west of Germany close to the Dutch border, approximately 130km to the north west of Koln, and around 25km to the south east of Nijmegen. The nearest airport is Düsseldorf (Weeze).

From the A57 motorway Koln to Goch, take exit 2 (Ausfahrt 2) Kleve/Goch-West and follow the signs for Kleve. After about 2km, turn left onto the B504 and follow the directions for Kranenburg. Continue for approximately 7km and then turn right (CWGC sign) onto the Grunewaldstrasse, in the direction of Kleve. Continue for around 3.5km and the cemetery can be found on the right.

Historical information

Reichswald Forest War Cemetery was created after the Second World War when burials were brought in from all over western Germany and it is the largest Commonwealth cemetery in the country.

Some of the members of the land forces buried there died in the advance through Reichswald Forest in February 1945. Others died crossing the Rhine, among them members of the airborne forces whose bodies were brought from Hamminkeln, where landings were made by the 6th Airborne Division from bases in England.

Some of the airmen buried in the cemetery lost their lives in supporting the advance into Germany but most died earlier in the war in the intensive air attacks over Germany. Their graves were brought in from cemeteries and isolated sites in the surrounding area.

There are now 7,594 Commonwealth servicemen of the Second World War buried or commemorated in the cemetery. 176 of the burials are unidentified. There are also 78 war graves of other nationalities, most of them Polish.

Special memorials to nine airmen are located at the east boundary wall, near plot 10. Further Special memorials to seven airmen are located within plot 31, near the Cross of Sacrifice. The cemetery was designed by Philip Hepworth.

KOHIMA WAR CEMETERY

Country: India
Identified casualties: 1,274

Location information

Kohima, the capital city of Nagaland state, is some 200km from the Indo-Burmese border (now known as the Indo-Myanmar border).

Kohima is best reached by air from Calcutta to Dimapur, or from Delhi to Dimapur, via Gauhati in Assam State and then by a winding road up the mountains. Kohima is 74km from Dimapur. It can also be reached by road from Gauhati – a long and difficult journey.

Kohima War Cemetery is situated on the left of the Imphal-Dimapur road (Highway 39), close to the centre of the town.

Visiting information

Kohima War Cemetery is open every day from 9am till 4pm. The cemetery is completely terraced with terrace levels ranging from 3–5m high, which makes wheelchair access to this site impossible.

Historical information

The Battle of Kohima was the turning point of the Japanese U-go offensive into India in 1944. The battle was fought in three stages from 4th April to 22nd June 1944 around the town of Kohima in north-east India.

From 3rd–16th April, the Japanese attempted to capture Kohima ridge, a feature which dominated the road and by which the besieged British and Indian troops were supplied. By mid-April, the small British force at Kohima was relieved.

From 18th April–13th May, British and Indian reinforcements counter-attacked to drive the Japanese from the positions they had captured. The Japanese abandoned the ridge at this point but continued to block the Kohima–Imphal road.

From 16th May–22nd June, British and Indian troops pursued the retreating Japanese and reopened the road. The battle ended on 22nd June, when British and Indian troops from Kohima and Imphal met at Milestone 109, ending the siege of Imphal.

Kohima has a large cemetery of 1,420 Allied war dead. It is maintained by the Commonwealth War Graves Commission. The cemetery lies on the slopes of Garrison Hill, in what was once the Deputy Commissioner's tennis court, which was the scene of the Battle of the Tennis Court. The epitaph carved on the memorial of the 2nd British Division in the cemetery has become world-famous as the Kohima Epitaph. The verse is attributed to John Maxwell Edmonds (1875–1958) and is reproduced here:

The Kohima

WHEN YOU GO HOME,

TELL THEM OF US AND SAY,

FOR THEIR TOMORROW,

WE GAVE OUR TODAY.

STATISTICAL INFORMATION

For those who enjoy statistics, I present some here.

Of the 49 names appearing on the First World War Memorial:

- all were from the Army except three who served in the Royal Navy

- 33 died in France or Flanders

- 13 in the Middle East

- 2 in European waters

- 1 in India.

Their regiments:

19 were with the Dorsetshire Regiment, 5 with the Hampshires, 3 with the Royal Field Artillery, 3 with the Devonshires and 2 with the Royal Navy. The balance of them were spread across a further 18 regiments

Their ages:

1 was 17	4 were 18	7 were 19	4 were 20
5 were 21	5 were 22	2 were 23	4 were 24
3 were 25	1 was 27	2 were 28	3 were 29

and 7 were 30 or more.

Years of passing:

3 died in 1914, 9 in 1915, 9 in 1916, 16 in 1917, 12 in 1918 and 3 after 1918.

Of the 26 names appearing on the Second World War Memorial:

15 were from the Army, 3 were Navy, 7 were RAF or RAFVR, and 1 was Home Guard

Their ages:

2 were 20	1 was 19	1 was 21	2 were 22	1 was 23	2 were 24
2 were 25	3 were 26	1 was 27	7 were in their 30's		3were older

Years of passing

4 died in 1940, 2 in 1941, 2 in 1942, 7 in 1943, 7 in 1944 and 4 in 1945.

INDEX OF NAMES

First World War

Adamson	Travers Farrant	8
Barber	Frederick Henry	22
Barrett	George Frederick	26
Bartlett	Bertie	3
Bartlett	Edward Charles	24
Beckett	George Herbert	13
Bradford	Edward	5
Bradford	Harry Alfred	15
Britten	Gilbert Sidney	20
Brown	Frederick George	7
Coward	Bertie	21
Coward	William	10
Crawshaw	Leslie	7
Dacombe	Percival Alfred	25
Dunford	Bertie	4
Flippant	Alfred Sidney	25
Gale	William George	16
Hallett	Walter James	11
Hames	Harry William	13
Hart	Edward Clifford	9
Hart	Ernest	18
Hart	George	17
Hart	Harry George	18

Hinton	Frank George	12
Hinton	Harry James	13
Hiscock	Edward James	17
Hopper	Frederick Walter	14
Kent	Ralph Edward Dawson	20
King	Ernest	6
King	John Albert	5
King	Laurence	16
Lawes	John Phillip	6
Longman	Victor Harry	19
Lush	Herbert	3
Lush	Thomas Eugene	10
Manston	Leonard Frederick	23
Maunsell	Edward Richard	8
Middleton	Herbert Charles	14
Pringle	Norman Douglas	5
Roberts	John Henry	4
Sanders	Arthur Edward	7
Shearing	Ernest Lewis	18
Shearing	George	12
Shephard	Frederick William	15
Squire	William Henry	22
Sutherland	Colin Allister	4
Vatcher	James Harry	23
Vincent	William Jefferson	24
Weston	Arthur	11
Woolridge	John	15

Second World War

Barrett	George Frederick	36
Bull	Alfred	34

Clark	James Alfred	39
Collier	John Laurence	40
Collins	Clifford John	43
Cox	James Frank	33
Fuller	Alfred Edward	38
Galliard	John Douglas	43
Hart	Arthur George	36
Hart	Norman John	39
Hunt	James Douglas	34
Jolliffe	Frederick Henry	37
Kenchington	Percy George	37
Kitchin	John Henry	35
March	RC	46
Miller	William Harry	42
Morey	Thomas Owen	41
Nott	Richard John William	32
Ramsay	John Basil	33
Read	Aubrey Charles George	40
Richmond	Frederick Tom	41
Robson	Clifford Allan	45
Shearing	Robert James	45
Smith	Frank Leonard	42
Smith	Leslie Norman	46
Young	Leslie John	38

ABOUT THE AUTHOR IAN DALE

Born in Manchester in 1945, Ian grew up mostly in Derbyshire before moving to London at the age of 13. In 1967 he married Irene and has two daughters and five grandchildren.

After an education in Science subjects (Chemistry, Physics, Zoology and Maths), Ian worked in biochemical research before embarking on a sales and management career, mainly in engineering in the threaded fastener industry.

In a complete change of lifestyle, in 1995 Ian bought a village Post Office in Somerset. He sold it in 2001 as a going concern, notwithstanding the impending closure of so many of these shops since. Next was the purchase of a hardware and housewares shop in 2004 in Goring-upon-Thames, Oxfordshire. This was sold in 2010 so Ian could retire. Both shops are still going strong under their new owners.

After moving with his wife to Dorset in 2011, Ian joined the Royal British Legion and the following year became Branch Treasurer at the Ferndown Branch, and Dorset County Treasurer in 2016.